SOUTHERN REGION ENGINEMAN

Life as an Engine Cleaner, Fireman and Passed Fireman at Nine Elms and Feltham 1957 - 1966

Includes firing on Sir Winston Churchill's Funeral Train

James (Jim) Lester

N.B.

ISBN 978-1-906419-27-1

First published in 2009 by Kevin Robertson
under the **NOODLE BOOKS** imprint
PO Box 279
Corhampton
SOUTHAMPTON
SO32 3ZX

www.kevinrobertsonbooks.co.uk

Printed in England by The Information Press

Front cover - *Platform 11 Waterloo, Saturday 30th January 1965, awaiting time to back onto the special train.* S. Stonestreet

Rear cover - *'Into the Night' reproduced by kind permission of Philip D. Hawkins GRA.* The picture is available as a Limited Edition Fine Art Print online at www.quicksilverpublishing.co.uk or call 01626 773288. To contact the artist email info@philiphawkins.co.uk or www.philiphawkins.co.uk or telephone 01626 862950.

DEDICATION

As the years have passed since the end of steam we have lost many of the fine men with whom we worked and for that reason I want to dedicate these pages to them all. On the occasions that we old Southern Enginemen meet and talk of times gone by their names are often mentioned nostalgically with genuine warmth and affection.

'God Bless Them All'

Note - all unaccredited photographs are from the author's collection.

Contents

INTRODUCTION

My own steam experiences, recorded here in SOUTHERN REGION ENGINEMAN, are indeed brief, in comparison with those that ought to be recorded by many of my likeminded more senior motive power friends and colleagues.

There are so many personal accounts that could be written by worthier men and thereby shared with those of us who have continued to be fascinated by the age of steam. Perhaps this modest narrative will stimulate others to do the same and record their life and times. I sincerely hope so.

James (Jim) Lester

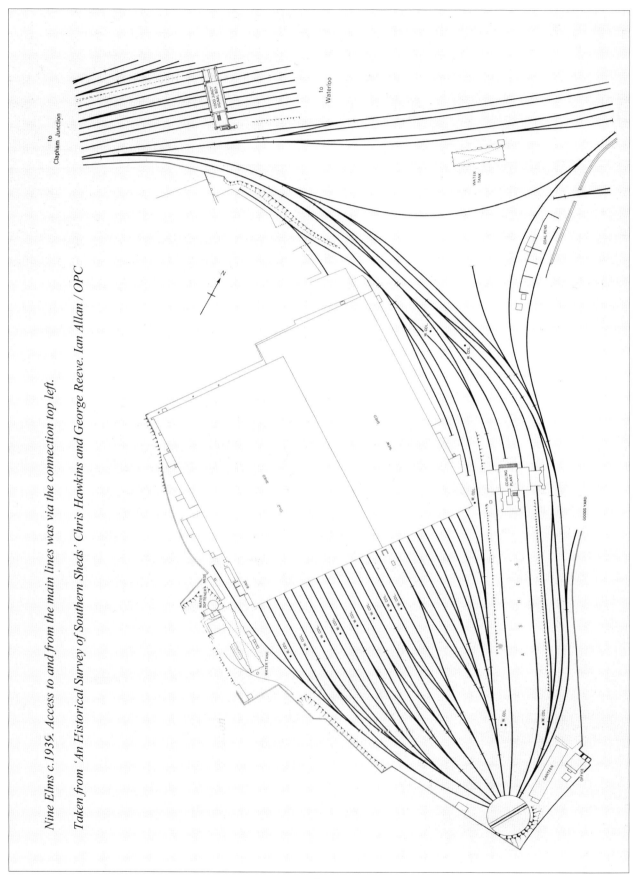

Nine Elms c.1935. Access to and from the main lines was via the connection top left.

Taken from 'An Historical Survey of Southern Sheds' Chris Hawkins and George Reeve. Ian Allan / OPC

Chapter 1

EARLY DAYS ENGINE CLEANING

Initial attempts to join the Southern Region's Motive Power Department at both Guildford and Feltham depots in 1957 failed, due to there being no vacancies for locomotive cleaners at that time. However, having been informed that vacancies did exist at Nine Elms, an interview at the depot, in South West London, was immediately arranged. After successfully passing the tests that I was set I then had to undergo a medical at the Southern Region's London Bridge medical centre. That I also happily passed.

The winter of 1957 was the beginning of a memorable railway career that began at the largest of the Southern Region's depots at Nine Elms, in Battersea. Through the years, smaller locomotive depots had been situated on a number of sites in close proximity to the original terminus of the London & Southampton

Railway at Vauxhall, dating back to 1838. As the railway had grown and developed, the original company became the London & South Western Railway, serving other large towns and cities in the southwest. Equally the depot grew and was finally relocated virtually where my story begins.

It must be remembered that this was one of the earliest main line railways to be built during the industrial revolution, funded initially by the businessmen of the day who required their variety of fresh produce and also imported goods from the south to reach the capital both in pristine condition and also as quickly as possible.

In 1923 the old London & South Western Railway gave way to the newly formed Southern Railway. Then some twenty-five years later it changed

As a young cleaner I would eagerly assist Charlie Anning, one of the depot's fire-lighters, looking after the many locomotives stabled in the shed. Here Class 'V', 4-4-0 (Schools), No 30902 'Wellington' receives my attention in 1958. Only after the electrification of the Southern's Eastern Section was Nine Elms again to house some of these marvellous locomotives following many years of absence.

Class 'WC', 4-6-2, 34097 'Holsworthy' stands in No. 11 road at Nine Elms in 1958 after recently being transferred from the Eastern Section. Doug Smith, on the right, and another cleaner colleague are seen on the footplate.

yet again, this time becoming the Southern Region of British Railways, consequent upon nationalisation in 1948.

Travelling from my home in Chertsey to Nine Elms depot was normally made via Weybridge. The old 'NOL' two-car sets that had been on the line since electrification in the mid-1930s had only just disappeared before I started work, being replaced with the 1950's EPB stock. However, from Weybridge, a mixture of 'HAL' and 'BIL' units formed the trains from Portsmouth and Alton to Waterloo in those days. The route to London via Staines was sometimes a good back-up, certainly when a late-running down service to Weybridge wasn't going to make the connection up to Waterloo. The nearest stations to Nine Elms were either Vauxhall or Queen's Road Battersea, with access to the depot at the end of Brooklands Road, just off the Wandsworth Road.

On the first day, I booked-on at the Time Office along with three other new entrants. We were taken to the stores at the bottom of number one road where we were equipped with two sets of overalls and a grease-top hat. We were then taken through the shed and across the twenty-five tracks that provided the maintenance and stabling points for all the locomotives. Ten tracks were in the 'New' shed, and fifteen in the 'Old' shed, the latter of which was only half-roofed due to un-repaired second-world war damage.

The interior of the cleaner's cabin, that was situated along-side twenty-five road, was like a step back in time. Dickensian did not really describe the scene as we entered the cabin for the first time. The early shift cleaners were sat there, eating their sandwiches with mugs of steaming tea, which seemed to me liken to the urchins associated with the Oliver Twist characters of Fagin and Bill Sykes.

Without due ceremony or introduction, Bill Clifton, the Cleaner Foreman, set us immediately to work and I was dispatched along with Bob Payne, a more senior cleaner in 1957, to learn the ropes. Nine Elms-allocated re-built Class 'Merchant Navy', 4-6-2, No. 35017 *'Belgian Marine'* was the very first locomotive that I cleaned on my first day. I remember well climbing into the driving cab after the cleaning had ceased, marvelling at the array of footplate controls and the size of the firebox. Only months before I had been observing the passing of such locomotives, hauling trains like the 'Atlantic Coast Express' and 'The Royal Wessex' from my favoured vantage point at Weybridge and now here I was, actually working on the very same locomotives.

Almost nine months cleaning now lay ahead, before my sixteenth birthday and the opportunity of taking my 'Fireman' examination. It was also during this period a steep learning curve was encountered. Doug Smith was another of the three cleaners who had started with me that day and we immediately became friends. To the others we were both considered 'country bumpkins', due to the fact that we both lived outside London. As I indicated earlier, I lived in Chertsey and Doug was from Effingham, his father then being a signalman at Surbiton.

Nine Elms certainly had a variety of locomotives as I recall. Whilst its primary fleet of main line engines consisted of examples of both the original and rebuilt Bulleid classes, 'Merchant Navy', 'West Country' / 'Battle of Britain' pacifics, a number of Maunsell 4-6-0 locomotives, Class 'LN' and 'N15' were still to be seen on shed. By then, only three of the

original sixteen 'Lord Nelson' locomotives were now allocated to Nine Elms, Nos 30858 *'Lord Duncan'*, 30859 *'Lord Hood'* and 30860 *'Lord Hawke'*. All, I recall, engines that I regularly cleaned in 1958. I remember well when working alone on one of them, having climbed up onto the handrail to clean the top of the boiler, I slipped and fell to the ground. I struck the running plate during my fall and then landed heavily on the brick paved walkway, right on top of my pile of cotton waste cleaning material that I had fortunately placed next to the locomotive. Although winded and slightly bruised, I realised later just how lucky I had been that day

I mentioned earlier, the Maunsell Class 'N15' 4-6-0 locomotives were still evident at the time and occasionally they could be seen performing main line duties particularly during the summer months when traffic demands were high. The 'King Arthur's were indeed a special engine and I have fond recollections of them and their legendary names. The fact that they were no longer involved in regular principal train operation had downgraded their status somewhat; cleaning them was thus not seen as a priority. However Doug and I would occasionally be given one of the depot's allocated locomotives to spruce up, either No 30763 *'Sir Bors De Ganis'*, 30770 *'Sir Prianius'*, 30771 *'Sir Sagramore'*,

Nine Elms allocated Class 'LN', 4-6-0, No. 30858, 'Lord Duncan' stands outside Bournemouth shed ahead of Class 'N15', 4-6-0, No. 30764 'Sir Gawain' in April 1958.

Class 'N15' 4-6-0 No 30771 'Sir Sagramore', stands in the un-roofed part of the 'old' 1889 shed. Still in good condition, I remember how proud I felt to be firing to these locomotives down to my hometown on the 'Chertsey Goods'.

30774 'Sir Gaheris', 30778 'Sir Pelleas' or 30779 'Sir Colgrevance'.

Among the other interesting locomotives to be seen were some of the last of the Urie 'H15' 4-6-0 class, built by the LSWR in 1914. Sadly I recall in later years, preparing one for her last run, 'light engine' to Eastleigh for scrapping. My Driver on this occasion was Bill Turner, later to become my regular mate, and he mentioned that this was the end for the 'old girl'. Alas she was in pretty poor condition when we climbed on to the footplate that fateful day, but we gave her a fine send off. During preparation we cleaned the boiler front, the windows and gauge glasses, rubbed up the brass and copper and hosed her down. She looked an absolute picture before departing on her last day. As I write these words I still remember just how I felt at that time; it was like losing an old friend.

Equally a number of LSWR Drummond engines were still employed for a variety of duties. The class 'M7' 0-4-4T were to be seen on the empty stock workings between Clapham Yard and Waterloo. Occasionally, in the summer months, they would be used to take any surplus rakes of coaches around to the sidings at Walton for berthing, thereby easing the demand on Clapham Yard. Normally these workings would be routed via Brentford and Staines, water invariably being taken en-route, at either Staines in the down loop, or sometimes at Chertsey. We also had three class '700' 0-6-0 locomotives, No's 30694, 30699 and 30701. These provided the motive power for some freight and fish turns down to Woking, also milk tank transferral to Morden milk depot from Clapham - Kensington sidings. The last of the Drummond locomotives that we had, were three fine 'T9', 4-4-0s, Nos 30718, 30719 and 30338. These had been tremendous engines in their time and could still be seen, some sixty years after being introduced, on the line from

London to Padstow and Plymouth part of the 'Withered Arm' in 1958.

There were also a number of 'Brighton' Class 'E4' 0-6-2T on shed and these would be used to perform shed shunting duties as well as ensuring the provision of coal wagon supplies to the enormous hopper adjacent to the depot. A weekly shunting turn, at the then busy Wimbledon West Yard, provided another duty for these large radial tank engines.

I recorded working on No 32500, she was in beautiful condition having recently returned from works resplendent in her new paintwork, whilst No 32473 (now on the Bluebell Railway) was another regular on this duty. Others members of the E4 class that I worked at that time, in the late 1950s, were 32486/87/93/97 and 32560/63.

'Chatham' motive power was meagrely represented by some Class 'U' locomotives, namely Nos 31617, 31621, 31624 and 31634. These 'Moguls' were extremely popular with crews and could be found throughout the Southern Region from Kent to the extremities of Cornwall.

In the nine months that I was engaged in cleaning, a serious incident occurred that caused quite a stir in the depot. A royal train was to run from Waterloo to Southampton with Class 'V' (Schools), No. 30906 'Sherborne' to provide the motive power on the day. Naturally one of the best of the class was selected for the prestigious duty and maintenance work on the designated locomotive was evident for a number of days leading up to the event.

Cleaners were personally supervised on these occasions to ensure that an immaculate locomotive was turned out, befitting the duty to be performed. On the actual day the locomotive was meticulously prepared and left the shed on time, bound for Waterloo, looking absolutely splendid. A number of the depot's

management had positioned themselves in the yard opposite to the main line, to watch the passing of the Royal Train after its departure from Waterloo. However an urgent phone call was received with a message, that was immediately relayed to the observers in the yard. This was that the locomotive had failed completely at Vauxhall. Naturally this was at first treated as a joke, that is until the gravity of the situation was fully realised. A standby engine had already been dispatched to Woking in the event of any unforeseen problems occurring but it could not be recalled in time. Only one other locomotive of the same class, No. 30907 'Dulwich', was in the depot and so it was hastily prepared. In comparison, this locomotive was in a filthy condition having received scant cleaning attention for many months. The aftermath of this event was exceedingly embarrassing, not only for the Nine Elms depot management, but for the South Western's Divisional Offices at Worple Road, Wimbledon. Subsequently an inquiry was implemented and due to the evidence found, after the locomotive was stripped down at the depot, sabotage was considered to be the likely cause. Thereafter the police interviewed everyone who had any involvement

'V' No 30906 'Sherborne' in happier times. The engine was allocated to Nine Elms from June 1957 until March 1960.
SOUTHERN-IMAGES

From *The Railway Magazine* - September 1958.

On August 7th, at about 9.00 am, No 30906 'Sherborne', broke down near Vauxhall when backing on to the Royal Train, composed of Pullman cars, which was taking the Queen from Waterloo to Southampton. The relief engine, No 30907 'Dulwich', was hurriedly summoned from Nine Elms and the special left on time, at 10.00. No 30906, the failure of which was stated to be because of a 'defective cylinder', blocked the up main line for nearly an hour.

The *Railway Observer* commenting on the same incident, reported the recalcitrant No 30906 was eventually propelled clear by a following empty steam train.

in the preparation of the locomotive. However the culprits, if indeed there were any, were never identified. It would appear that six-inch nails were found to have disastrously damaged the locomotives piston valves and thus wrecked the front end. It was further determined that these nails had entered the steam chest via the chimney and blast-pipe. Work on the 'new' shed roof was in progress at the time and it was remotely possible that the nails, being used for the repair work, had accidentally dropped into the smoke-box by the workmen above. I guess we will never really know the truth, but stranger things have happened!

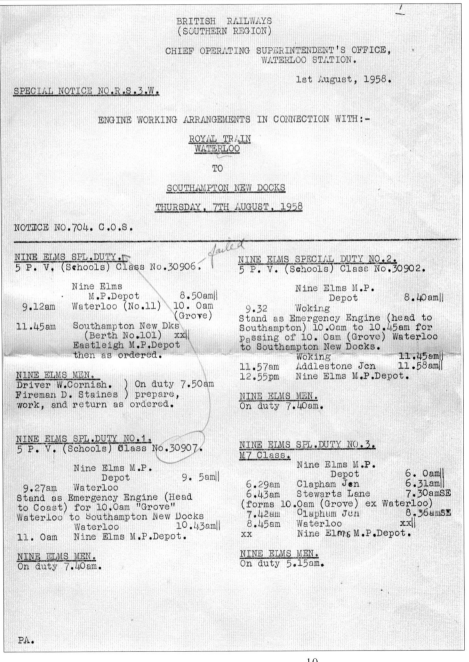

Special traffic notice for the Royal Train Working of 7th August 1958. As was the practice at the time, these workings were always designated with the codeword 'Grove'.

As mentioned in the text, although not prepared externally, 30907 was the official stand-by engine at Nine Elms, No 30902 having already been despatched to Woking. Further standby engines were ready at Basingstoke, No 30904, and Eastleigh, 30853. In the event 30907 worked through.

Driver Bill Cornish and Fireman Doug Stainer (note the incorrect spelling on the special notice) were in charge, with the train formed of four vehicles, corridor luggage van No 2351, Pullman brake, 'Isle of Thanet' (brake leading), Pullman car 'Aries' - for the Royal Party, and Pullman brake 'Minerva' (brake trailing). Inspector Gayland, a regular man on such workings, also travelled on the train.

My sixteenth birthday could not come too soon. in order that I could progress to 'Passed Cleaner' status. This would involve passing an examination at the Guildford Training School for Firemen, located in a small building adjacent to the locomotive disposal pits at Guildford depot. However, in the meantime I had to be patient and learn as much as possible about the locomotive as well as the contents of the 1950 Rule Book.

During this period I also got to know Driver Don King and his Fireman Alan Wilton, likewise Driver Jim Roberts and his Fireman Arthur Baker and I would assist them whenever the chance allowed. Then one day Arthur Baker invited me to accompany them, 'unofficially', on the footplate of the 09.00 am Waterloo - Salisbury - Exeter service. This then became a regular occurrence whenever they had the turn and when my shift allowed me to take the opportunity. The return working from Salisbury was an 'All Stations' service to Woking, then on to Waterloo, usually hauled by one of Salisbury's own long serving 'N15' locomotives or some times a Maunsell Class 'S15'. On the return leg, I would fire the locomotive as far as Woking. Arthur would instruct me on the finer points of firing and boiler control and, once I had mastered the art of firing and the balance required, it became a great pleasure to be totally in charge without any instruction necessary. Equally Alan Wilton, who was a great authority on Bulleid locomotives, invited me on several footplate trips 'down the main'. When later I eventually did become a 'Passed Cleaner' and was called upon to work an occasional mainline duty, these earlier experiences gave me the confidence required and similarly stood me in good stead throughout my career.

Driver Peter Steward is seen here on Nine Elms allocated 'Standard Class '' 4-6-0, No 73111, waiting at Waterloo whilst performing No 73 Duty in 1959 - see overleaf. At sixteen, and now a 'Passed Cleaner', I was now officially on the roster although not appointed as a Fireman, which was a bone of contention at the time.

(Nine Elms duty No 73 was altered post 1956 to include additional empty stock workings).

NINE ELMS DUTY No. 73
5 P/5 F (B.R. Standard)

MONDAYS ONLY

Stabled off No. 73, **Saturday.**

—	Basingstoke Loco.	... 5.30 a.m. ‖	
**	Barton Mill Sdgs.	...	** E
**	Basingstoke	... ...	—
	C—Shunting 5.40 a.m. to 6.10 a.m.		
—	Basingstoke	... 6.37 a.m.	P
		... 9.45 a.m.	E
8. 8 a.m.	Waterloo	... ** ‖	
9.55 a.m.	Clapham Jc.	... ...	—
**	Nine Elms	...	

FRIDAYS EXCEPTED.

—	Nine Elms Loco.	... 9.35 p.m. ‖	
9.50 p.m.	Nine Elms Goods	...10.40 p.m.	F

MONDAYS EXCEPTED. ...

7.44 a.m.	Weymouth... ...	... ** ‖	
**	W.R. Loco.	... 9. 0 a.m. ‖	
**	Weymouth...	... 9.20 a.m.	P
10.27 a.m.	Bournemouth Ctl.	...10.29 a.m. ‖	
**	Loco. Yard	... ...	—

Stable for No. 74.

FRIDAYS ONLY.

—	Nine Elms Loco.	... 9.35 p.m. ‖	
9.50 p.m.	Nine Elms Goods	...10.40 p.m.	F
4.21 a.m.	Poole	... 5. 5 a.m.	F

and work No. 73 **Sat.**

Basingstoke Men.

M.O.—Off No. 240, prepare for 5.30 a.m. ‖

Feltham Men.

M.O.—Off No. 116 relieve 5.30 a.m., work and relieved at Waterloo 8.8 a.m., and home passenger.

Nine Elms Men.

1st set (**M.O.**) on duty 7.38 a.m., relieve 8.8 a.m., work and dispose.

Off No. 72, prepare and train for 10.40 p.m.

NINE ELMS DUTY No. 73—continued.

Eastleigh Men.

Off No. 32, relieve Nine Elms 10.0 p.m., relieved at Southampton Ctl. 1.36 a.m., home per lorry.

Bournemouth Men.

1st set on duty 11.12 p.m. pass. to Southampton Ctl. relieve 1.36 a.m., work and relieved at Poole 4.45 a.m. pass. per 5.32 a.m. Branksome and assist requirements No. 3 duty.

2nd set (**M.X.**) on duty 2.35 a.m., dispose No. 424, passenger per No. 381 duty engine to Poole, relieve at 4.45 a.m., work and relieved in Depot.

M.X.—No. 1 P. & D. men dispose.

[continued.

73

Chapter 2

PASSED CLEANER EXPERIENCES

On reaching the age of sixteen in September 1958, I received notice to attend a Fireman's training course at Guildford for a single week of tuition. Arriving with my colleagues on the Monday morning, we made our way across the foot-crossing at the tunnel end of the station and then presented ourselves to Inspector George Bolland at the Training School. Initially he wanted to find out what we had learned during the period we had spent cleaning, and did this by asking us numerous questions. We were then issued with a British Transport Commission publication – 'Handbook for Railway Steam Locomotive Enginemen' – dated 1957. I still have it today and treasure the now rather dog-eared but priceless link to the past and the days of steam.

We certainly learned a great deal during that short time at Guildford and then, at the end of the week, Mr Bolland duly informed us that we had all passed both the theory and practical examination. It was indeed a special moment, something that I'd wanted to achieve since my interest in railways first began in the late 1940s and early 1950s. During my Ian Allan ABC Spotting days dating back to those times I'd recorded and studied numerous classes of Southern locomotives that I had observed, all of which had influenced me in my chosen career.

Normally once you had passed the firing examination, you would be booked as a Fireman on an 'As Required' basis on the daily alteration sheet as an upgrade from cleaning to firing. Each firing turn worked would be recorded and as such you would receive more money having accumulated specific numbers of turns. However, whilst this method of working was a 'National Agreement' on British Railways the requirement for firemen at Nine Elms was particularly high and I never

This was a typical late 1950's scene at Guildford MPD. A Bulleid 'Q1', 0-6-0 No 33008, Urie 'S15', 4-6-0' No. 30515 and two Maunsell locomotives, a 'V', 4-4-0, No. 30913 'Christ's Hospital' and a 'U' 2-6-0, are seen here standing on the back road. The Training School was located just the other side of these locomotives. Later during our week's tuition, we had to clean smoke-boxes, remove clinker from the fireboxes and rake out ash-pans on similar engines.

N. Hampshere

cleaned another locomotive all the time I was a 'Passed Cleaner'.

My first allocated 'firing' turns were in the 'Table Gang' with a regular Driver, Len Trigg. Len was on this work as he had failed his medical as an electric Driver at Hampton Court. The gang worked a three shift basis, 6.00am – 2.00pm, 2.00pm – 10.00pm and 10.00pm – 6.00am and, even at the age of sixteen, I was booked to work all three shifts. The duties basically consisted of moving locomotives that had been left on the disposal pit, after any necessary work had been completed and then placing them in the respective shed roads according to their next diagrammed duty or shed maintenance requirement.

Sometimes these locomotives had no fire in them, consequently the steam pressure would be low, depending on the condition that the last fireman had left the boiler. In these circumstances great care was needed when moving, as the brake effort would be affected by the lack of pressure. This applied not only to the steam brake, but also the vacuum brake, due to the inability to create the full twenty-one inches of vacuum normally required, thus again reducing the brake force. There was always a shunting engine available to move the 'dead' engines out of the shed and this required the co-operation of the shed staff in general. Just one locomotive found with a red 'Not to be Moved' board located on a lamp bracket could cause delay, requiring the person who placed the board in position being found to remove it!

Locomotives were constantly moved from road to road in the shed to release others going into traffic after the completion of various regular maintenance regimes. Boiler washouts were one such frequent requirement, brick arch and fire-bar replacement, tube cleaning, brake-block replacements, gland packing, clacks, injectors, vacuum ejectors, steam brakes were but some of the continuing work that would be undertaken by the specialist workforce in the shed. More serious defects could not always be dealt with at the depot, not even one the size of Nine Elms, and as such would require 'works' intervention down at Eastleigh.

The system of booking locomotive defects was the responsibility of the driver. On returning to the depot, a repair card would be completed by him, recording the maintenance that was deemed necessary. It was equally the responsibility of the fireman to bring to the attention of the driver any defects that he had himself observed, particularly those seen in the firebox or in the smoke-box during the cleaning process. Sometimes the driver would need to 'test' the locomotive by setting the big-end and valve gear in a certain positions and then checking for any excessive movement from the ground whilst the fireman applied steam with the brakes on. This could reveal big or small

end wear, axle-box problems, even a loose cylinder on occasions.

After some months in the 'Table Gang' I was promoted to the 'Coal Road Shunter' Link. During my time in this link I worked with Driver Jack Roberts, a lovely old chap. There were only two shifts in the link, early and late with no night work. Alec Mane was the other driver on the opposite shift and he and his mate would relieve us about 1.30 pm when we were early turn. We always had one of the depot's 'E4' 0-6-2T, large radial tank engines on this turn and always kept her clean and tidy. The Westinghouse air brake provided a good brake force on the six-coupled locomotive for shunting, plus it had the adhesion required to lift the empty coal wagons out of the depot on our daily trip to Nine Elms Goods Yard, located on the other side of the main line, accessed via the two Viaduct signal-boxes that controlled movements from one yard to the other. On the return trip, we would bring back the fully loaded coal wagons ready to replenish the coal supply to the huge hopper. From the 'E4's footplate one could watch all the locomotives entering and departing the depot during the day, it was a sight that fascinated me during the early summer months of 1959. Whilst the early shift required Jack and I to prepare the locomotive in the morning for the day's work ahead, on the late shift we simply disposed of it. On most occasions I would have to save the fire, this required the clinker to be removed leaving a small, but adequate, clean fire in the locomotive over night ready for the next day. As I previously mentioned, when locomotives were booked 'shed-days', the fire would be removed in order that the periodical maintenance work could be carried out. On the late shift, after this particular disposal was completed, our last duty would be to relieve an Eastleigh crew on an incoming Class 'Lord Nelson' 4-6-0, while they went and had their meal break. During the short period that it was in the depot, we would take on coal, turn the locomotive and fill the tender with water. I would remove any large deposits of clinker from the fire-box, then build up the fire in readiness for the 'Down Mail' working. Thinking back, these were some of the first of the large express class locomotives that I actually worked on in the early part of 1959.

After leaving Jack Roberts and the 'Coal Road Shunter' duties to my replacement fireman, I was promoted this time into the '6B' link, firing to Jim Rebbeck. Jim was himself a young driver, who originated from Salisbury and who had moved to Nine Elms to gain promotion. The confines of the shed were occasionally left behind now, as the duties in this small link included a late afternoon shunting turn at Raynes Park Goods. At the end of the evening peak service, on completion of shunting duties in the local yard, we would work back to Nine Elms Goods via Wimbledon

Class 'M7', 0-4-4T, N. 30319, stands in Nine Elms 'old' shed of 1889 in 1958. My friend Robin Bell is seen on the footplate of this almost 60 year-old locomotive. In 1900 it had been built but a few hundred yards away when Nine Elms Works was still operational and for a cost of £1,650. The engine was eventually withdrawn from service in 1960.

West Yard. The motive power on this turn was usually one of the three Bulleid Class 'Q1' 0-6-0 locomotives we had, Nos 33015, 33017 or 33038.

Later that same year I briefly fired to David Duncan Davis, 'DD', as he was known at the depot. Dave was one of the younger Nine Elms appointed drivers, who had been through all the links as a fireman, something that in reality faced me in 1958. It was a somewhat short experience working with him, but later in life Dave would relate to others quite proudly that I was his first regular mate. Most of the duties we performed were the usual preparation and disposal of locomotives, with occasional empty coaching stock. It is interesting to record that during this brief period there was a week's work on 'N15', No 30450 *'Sir Kay'*, doing several trips working between Clapham Yard and Waterloo. It may not sound much now, but I recall it was a great feeling running into Waterloo, albeit only from Clapham, with a 'King Arthur' class engine on the front of the train at the age of sixteen!

Promotion through the various links followed and on each occasion another rung of the ladder was climbed and the quality of the work gradually improved, as did my knowledge of locomotives and firing duties. Throughout its long history, Nine Elms depot had always been managed on the basis of 'senior men, senior work' and this rule was sacrosanct. Naturally by this token, the 'Top Link' had the best of the depot's work and I looked forward to the day when I too would attain a position in the premier link.

Around the time I joined the railways there had been a setback to the normal progression of both junior drivers and firemen alike. This came about due to the dieselisation of shunting duties at both Clapham Yard and Nine Elms Goods and where previously numerous steam locomotives crews had been gainfully employed. These shunting turns were recorded in 'Nine Elms Engineman', the book that Bert Hooker wrote so

descriptively when recalling his days at Nine Elms. The advent of the 350hp diesel shunting locomotives thus reduced the need for firemen and also reduced the requirement of some drivers. In addition, other young Firemen who had been away doing their two years 'National Service' were now returning and taking up their correct link position. Those junior to them were reduced to lower positions in the links, some even going back to cleaning. This was nothing new in the industry, for many of the country's railway companies had operated like this for many years. Conversely, in the summer months the manpower requirement was immense, although in winter men were regularly demoted each year. Indeed in certain cases men in their fifties were still on regular firing duties at other depots, particularly in the West of England. I recall, whilst I was in the 'Top Link' at the age of twenty-two, that my regular relief at Salisbury was an Exmouth Junction fireman in his late forties. I equally remember an elderly Branksome fireman, no doubt in his fifties, shovelling my coal forward in the little Dorset depot prior to our return journey to London from Bournemouth West.

Fortunately things did eventually settle down and in late 1959 I was again on the move, this time into No. 6 Link. A. E. (Dickie) Budd was my new driver this time, a genial chap who had started his railway career early in 1938 and been through all the Nine Elms links as a fireman. No. 6 link contained the odd freight working to Feltham Yard and the 'Chertsey' Goods. The booked locomotive used on the latter duty was normally one our Class N15s that I referred to previously. This was a rather special duty for me, so I have taken the time to describe the work involved on the turn.

After signing on at 1.45am for No 21 Duty we would prepare the locomotive, normally one of our Class 'N15' 4-6-0s and then would run light engine at 2.45 am to Nine Elm Goods Yard and, on arriving at Top Yard, would drop back on to the wagons that made

NINE ELMS DUTY No. 21.

5 P. (N.15 Class)

—	Nine Elms Loco. ...	2.45 a.m.	‖
3. 0 a.m.	Nine Elms Goods ...	3.30 a.m.	F
5.45 a.m.	Weybridge ...	6.15 a.m.	F
6.49 a.m.	Chertsey	7.10 a.m.	‖
7.30 a.m.	Woking	8.45 a.m.	P
9.28 a.m.	Basingstoke ...	10.45 a.m.	P
11.52 a.m.	Salisbury	11.57 a.m.	E
**	West Sidings ...	12. 5 p.m.	‖
12.10 p.m.	Loco. Yard ...	8.25 p.m.	‖
**	Salisbury	9. 2 p.m.	M
	(5.35 p.m. ex Yeovil)		
	(via E. Putney.)		
11.36 p.m.	Clapham Jc.	**	‖
**	Nine Elms	—	

Nine Elms Men.

1st set on duty 1.45 a.m., relieved at Woking at 8.30 a.m. and home pass.

Eastleigh Men.

M.O.—Off No. 108, relieve Woking 8.30 a.m. work and relieved Basingstoke 9.28 a.m., then relieve No. 68 at 9.58 a.m.

Basingstoke Men.

M.X.—Off No. 110, relieve at Woking 8.30 a.m. and relief at Basingstoke 9.28 a.m.

Eastleigh Men.

Off No. 393, relieve at Basingstoke at 9.28 a.m. work and relieved in Salisbury Loco., relieve No. 443 at 12.30 p.m., work and relieved at Eastleigh at 1.53 p.m., then dispose No. 303.

Salisbury Men.

Off No. 412 (W) (M.O.), No. 414/414A (W) (M.X.), dispose then prepare No. 441.

Off No. 435, prepare for 8.25 p.m.‖.

1st set on duty 8.10 p.m., relieved at Woking 10.50 p.m. then relieve No. 441 at 12.35 a.m., work and relieved at Salisbury 4.7 a.m.

Nine Elms Men.

Off No. 75, relieve at Woking 10.50 p.m., work and dispose and as ordered.

---

up our train. This normally consisted of an assortment of sixty or more loose-coupled vehicles that sometimes required us to shunt making up the full train, after which we departed at 3.30 am Once under way, we would draw up to the signal on the middle road at Queens Road Battersea, where we would cross over onto the 'Down Main Local' towards West London Junction. Here it was essential to exchange hand lamp signals with the guard to ensure all the train was intact. Incidentally, there wasn't actually a junction at West London at the time, for the original track layout had been abandoned many years ago. However in the 1990s it was reinstated for the 'Eurostar' trains to travel empty to their new depot at North Pole International.

We would then call in at Wimbledon West Yard, leaving a portion of the train behind, before continuing on to Surbiton where the same process took place. Next stop was Walton Yard where, after finally setting the vans back in the shed, a welcome can of tea was freshly brewed using the signalman's kettle. After the steam hauled 4.45 am Waterloo to Woking had departed from the station, we were signalled out of the yard as soon as it was clear of Oatlands, a small intermediate signal-box further down the line. Arriving at Weybridge, we would set back from the Down Local line, across the two fast lines, on to the 'Up Local' where we would be signalled into the small yard opposite the signal-box. I remember early one summer morning, after shunting the yard, we propelled our train out of the sidings into the bay at Weybridge. On this particular occasion we had a clean locomotive No 30779 'Sir Colgrevance', it looked quite a sight standing there, with our somewhat reduced freight train as we now waited for the old LSWR lower quadrant signal to clear. This signal would allow our progress on towards Addlestone Junction and the yards at Addlestone and Chertsey. Later, once the shunting was completed at the last of these destinations, the customary tail lamp was attached and the head-code changed in readiness for a tender first light-engine run back to Weybridge, where we would be signalled out on to the 'Up Local' line. After stopping and yet another change of head-code and tail-lamp and, with the ground signal 'off', we would cross on to the 'Down Fast' line and for the first time that day 'lively' make our way down to Woking. Eventually we would drop back into the bay platform and take water, after which we would ease back onto some empty stock and couple on. A little later Basingstoke men would relieve us who would then take the train 'All Stations' to Basingstoke.

As I mentioned earlier, work in the lower links at Nine Elms consisted of many hours preparing and disposing of locomotives, which in general terms was extremely hard work on most occasions. Whilst our ten allocated 1950s Derby-built 'Standard Class 5' locomotives, 73110 –73119, had self-cleaning smoke-boxes and rocking / drop grates all of which aided the fireman immeasurably, it must be remembered that almost all of the older Southern locomotives required intensive clinker-shovel work, some times in awful conditions. In particular the 'Lord Nelson' and original 'Merchant Navy' locomotives required excessive stamina to clean not only the large smoke-boxes but also

The first of the influx of WR 0-6-0 Pannier Tanks engines, No 9770, stands outside the Nine Elms 'new' shed' in the early 1960's.
Mike Roberts

the fireboxes, both of which were quite substantial in size. Without the rocking / drop grates, introduced only later on the re-built 'Merchant Navy' class, this was some of the most arduous work of shed work. In particular, I recall one day disposing of the engine off the Up 'Atlantic Coast Express'. Great care was always required when opening the smoke-box on a locomotive, particularly one that had just completed a round journey without any cleaning. After releasing the central dart, that retained the smoke-box door in an air-tight position, opening the door was an art of survival. Pull on the door and hang to it, such was the level of smoke-box char, for it would be at least two thirds full and would come cascading down onto the plate above the buffer beam, plus it was extremely hot, to say the least. Cleaning this alone would take a good thirty or forty minutes of continual shovelling. Once that was complete the real work began, namely removing all the clinker deposit from the fire-box. Yet again another rigorous period of shovelling, this time with the clinker shovel, possibly for an hour or more before finally the ash pan was approached.

This last task required entering the pit, normally from the tender end and, after making ones way forward to a point beneath the fire-box, raking out the accumulation of ash. It was always a dirty job and determining both the direction of the wind and the condition of the pit was essential before venturing under the locomotive. Sometimes water in the pit could be covered by a layer of smoke-box char giving the impression that it was OK to enter, invariably you learned the hard way, I certainly did, but then as you get older you get wiser!

In 1959 I witnessed the introduction of the '57XX' class 0-6-0PT locomotives from the Western Region, No 9770, ex-Plymouth Laira (83D), being the first of these locomotives to arrive at Nine Elms for

trials. Prior to arriving with us, it had been tested down at Folkestone Harbour. Others of the class that followed were all ex-Wales-based locomotives. We learned that some of the ageing Drummond 'M7's were to be replaced by these rather soul-less locomotives. When more of the class eventually arrived, I can't say that they endeared themselves to the great majority of the footplate fraternity. They were most uncomfortable and particularly awkward in every aspect. Conversely, they were certainly strong, for they would lift twelve or thirteen coaches with relative ease on the stock working between Waterloo and Clapham Yard. However, their final departure was not lamented. Their arrival also created quite a few brake-related incidents, due to the twenty-five inches of vacuum that the Western Region used.

Some trains leaving from Waterloo suffered from dragging brakes, caused by the fact that the empty stock brought into the terminal had more that the prescribed twenty-one inches of vacuum. As a consequence the train engine could not fully release the carriage brakes, due to the imbalance between the vacuum established in the rolling stock reservoirs being greater than that which could be created in the brake pipe.

I remember personally 'suffering' the rigours involved in this situation, when called upon to fire to 'Top Link' Driver Sam Mills on 66 Duty, the 5.39 pm to Salisbury, one January evening in 1959.

As soon as we departed from Waterloo with our train of eleven coaches, the trouble began immediately the banking engine 'dropped off' the rear at the top of the platform. Despite the fact that the locomotive, a 'Standard Class 5', No 73111, was driven extremely hard, we had barely attained 40 mph at Clapham Junction. Similar tardy progress was made all the way to Woking, where we eventually arrived both

Drummond 'M7', 0-4-4T, No 30123 stands in Clapham Yard waiting for the signal to depart with empty stock for Waterloo. Many of these locomotives were built at the original LSWR Nine Elms Works, that, after closure in 1909, became a covered Goods Sheds. This was when the locomotive works was transferred to Eastleigh.

rather late and a bit the worse for wear. Sam was immediately on the phone to the signalman and then organised the 'strings' to be pulled to destroy the excessive reservoir vacuum throughout the train. In the meantime, I toiled to restore the fire, water level and boiler pressure for our continued journey. On restarting the train from Woking, what a difference. We freely accelerated through the cutting at St Johns, easily climbing the bank on towards Pirbright Junction and Farnborough, our next stop. I believe the delay to the service that day perhaps highlighted the problem surrounding the introduction of these locomotives and consequently changes were implemented that improved the general situation.

Now the problem had been identified, the release 'strings' were regularly pulled on the empty stock whilst it stood in Waterloo. In addition the vacuum limit valves and pumps on the locomotives received closer attention in the shed.

The WR Pannier Tank engines were in their turn replaced some years later by the BR 'Standard Class 3' 2-6-2T engines, and I recall bringing one of them 'light engine' up to Nine Elms from Salisbury one night. Many of these locomotives had similarly become redundant from other depots and in general terms were a far more acceptable replacement locomotive. About the same time a Class 'H' 0-4-4T, No. 31326, was seen on shed for a trial period. However, I never had the opportunity of actually working on the locomotive although I had travelled behind members of the same class on many occasions on various branch lines in the South East.

On the 22nd February 1960 another move was imminent, this time into No 5 Link or the 'Dual Link' as it was known. I would also now be firing to Fred Elliott. No 5 was a rather large link, the drivers in which not only worked on steam, but also electric traction. In terms of the latter they would undertake complete electric turns of duty involving both suburban and some main line services. Whilst the driver was so engaged, allocated on a weekly basis within the link, his regular firemen would remain in the shed, to perform whatever duties became available. Understandably, it wasn't very long before I became disenchanted with this method of working, as it was back to the constant preparation and disposal of locomotives. The lack of a regular mate, plus the extremely un-social hours week after week and few running turns in the link, made me seriously consider my future at this point. An old cleaner friend of mine, Barry Mackett who lived at Norbiton, had earlier transferred from Nine Elms down the line to Feltham depot. We had kept in touch and he had described the difference in the work that lower link Firemen performed at Feltham. I made further enquiries about the work and the link position that I would take if I were to apply for promotion. Considering all things, I decided to apply for the position of fireman at the depot on the February vacancy list. In the meantime life as a 'Passed Cleaner' in No 5 Link continued much the same, however I now looked forward to a complete change of railway work.

Thus, at the end of March 1960, I received confirmation that I had been successful in my application and that I would take up the vacancy at Feltham on 4th April 1960. Leaving Nine Elms I wondered whether I had made the right decision. Only time would tell.

Chapter 3

FIREMAN & FELTHAM FREIGHT DAYS

Travelling to Feltham was certainly easier than to Nine Elms. However, there was still quite a substantial walk, in all weathers, from the station up the yard to the depot. Previously, on the occasions I had used the Staines route to travel to London, I would always observe the hump yards and the steam depot at the top end near Feltham Junction. Whilst at Nine Elms I had worked into Feltham Yard a few times, but was certainly not fully conversant with the general layout of the yard and locomotive movements in and around the depot.

I recall the last of the Adams 0-6-0 Class '0395' No 30567, built in 1883, that was allocated to the depot and finally withdrawn in October 1959. Two of Feltham's Class 'O2', 0-4-4T, Nos 30177 and 30179 were to be seen on shed on one occasion when we dropped onto one of the two disposal pit roads in 1959, alas also coming to the end of their working lives. At that time, all twenty of the Urie 1920s-built Class 'S15', 4-6-0, were allocated here, plus of course the Class 'H16' 4-6-2T, and the 'G16' 4-8-0T, the latter the only eight coupled LSWR locomotives ever built. Drummond engines were also to be found on shed, Class 'M7' 0-4-4T, and '700' 0-6-0's regular diagrammed, all of which I would work on in due course. In addition Feltham had also received a few transferred engines, including some ex-SECR Class 'C' 0-6-0. Following the electrification

on the 'South Eastern' section these engines had become surplus, indeed quite a few other SECR locomotives were to be seen on the 'South Western' metals for the same reason. Bulleid Class 'Q1' 0-6-0's made up the remainder of the depot allocation in 1960.

Rather oddly I equally discovered there were two ex-LBSCR Class 'C2X' 'Vulcan' 0-6-0, locomotives, Nos 32437 and 32438. The former gaining the nickname 'Sabrina' due to its double domed boiler and the connection with a rather large bosomed lady of that time. In addition to these we also had two Class 'E6' 0-6-2T Nos 32408 and 32416. Plenty of variety to look forward to in the coming months.

But I digress. Reporting to the main office, I established I would take my positioned in No 3 link from 2nd May and confirmed that my new driver would be Derek Leming, who, as it turned out, also lived at Chertsey. Later I learned that all the male members of the Leming family were railwaymen. Derek's father, who lived in the Chertsey station house, was a driver at EMU depot there, whilst Derek's brothers were all on the footplate. During the following years I met them all, it was indeed a pleasure knowing and working with them, a special family indeed.

Unlike at Nine Elms, I soon found out that until I reached 18, the earliest I could sign-on for rostered work at Feltham was 6.00 am. Similarly, the latest

Showing a few signs of wear and tear some forty-seven years later, my notification of appointment to Fireman at Feltham, dated the 30th March 1960. At the age of 17, this move enabled me to work on other classes of Southern locomotives predominantly used for freight working.

Class 'C2X' 0-6-0, No 32438, seen here at Shepperton, with Driver Derek Leming at the regulator. After shunting the small yard had been completed we are waiting in the platform to work back tender first to Twickenham.

finishing time must be no later than 10.00 pm. Whether indeed Lord Shaftesbury or William Wilberforce had any direct influence on this situation at Feltham I never did find out; whatever, I liked climbing up chimneys, or the equivalent of it in my time on the railways!

Compared with the sprawl of Nine Elms, Feltham depot was not particularly large, having just six through roads in the shed which also enabled locomotives to leave the depot from either end. The West End of the shed provided the motive power for freight trains routed to Portsmouth, Southampton, Salisbury and Reading, whilst East End supplied locomotives involved in the interchange freight operation that linked the Southern with the London Midland, Eastern and Western Regions. Trains to Nine Elms Goods would complete the internal services. At this time there was also still a healthy local freight service that would require all the station yards to be regularly visited by the daily 'pick-up goods'. This was some of the core work that I immediately found myself involved in, along with some of the transfer freight work to the other regions.

There was a general movement of other senior men in their respective links scheduled for the same time in May, so until that took place I had to remain 'spare'. Careful scrutiny of the alteration sheet at the end of the day was thus essential to correctly establish my next duty.

My second day at Feltham involved preparing a rather unusual locomotive, 'WD 2-8-0, No 90261. This, I learned, was on trial at the depot and was due to work down to Reading. I established later that the general opinion of these locomotives was they were not in any

way better than our existing 'S15' type from 1920. Despite the fact that the WDs were some twenty-three years their junior, being built in 1943. Later the same day I disposed of 'H16' 4-6-2T, No 30519, destined to be the start of many footplate experiences with this loco. The next week's work certainly made me feel confident that I had made the right decision to transfer, as I was firing to Feltham 'Top Link' driver, Bert Jayne on '700' 0-6-0, No 30689, working vans to Clapham Yard and returning later with a freight train from Nine Elms Goods. Bert was somewhat concerned at first that he didn't have his regular mate and was somewhat brusque when we turned the loco before leaving the depot for the West End. However once we got underway he mellowed, the fact that safety valves were humming away and the footplate was clean and tidy may have had some bearing on the matter. Whatever by the end of the day we were firm friends. Later in the week I found myself firing to Jack Mansey, another jovial character, this time on 'G6' 0-6-0T, No 30349 dating back to 1892. Even the shunting turns I found extremely interesting and recorded the daily events as they occurred.

After only a couple of weeks at the depot I had 'rough' trip with a Feltham freight bound for Woking and Guildford. This was with Driver Kench on a '700', No 30346. I must admit it rather dented my ego in respect to my considered opinion that I had mastered the art of firing to 'Drummond' locomotives. To try and improve matters, I decided to clean the fire at Guildford and make amends on the return trip, quite a task in the short time available. However it paid dividends and honour was duly restored. I remember personally how it was always a pleasure to get the best out of the engines

Representatives of the LBSCR, SE&CR and LSWR stand together just outside the shed at Feltham. 'E6' 0-6-2T No 32408; a 'C' 0-6-0 and a Urie 'S15' 4-6-0. Two of the 'E6' locomotives, No 32416 being the other, were at Feltham during my time there. They were typical "Brighton" engines and had an air-assisted reverser to help shunting. Note the unusual safety valves, set across the boiler and the extended lamp brackets over the buffer beam.

that I fired, particularly the older ones dating back to the late 1890s and early 1900s.

The month of May soon arrived and I took my place in No. 3 Link with Derek Leming and soon began to rotate through the rostered turns that made up the work content in this gang. Naturally there was still a small proportion of shed-based work on preparation and disposal of the various locomotives that required servicing, plus of course the shed and yard shunting that I mentioned earlier. The Feltham depot coal hopper certainly did not need a dedicated locomotive to provide a constant supply of fuel as did the one at Nine Elms.

Very soon I became familiar with the Wainwright 'C' 0-6-0 locomotives and on my third week recorded working local freight trains and shunting turns in Twickenham and Richmond yards on 31037, 31054 and 31113. These had previously based at Ashford and Hither Green depots.

From my early interest in railways I had always been fascinated by the older LSWR locomotives, many of them still to be seen on the Southern in the early 1950's. Guildford was a favourite haunt of mine and like Feltham, the depot had a number of the surviving Adams Class '0395' 0-6-0s. Originally seventy engines made up the class, but fifty were sent to the Middle East during the First World War never to return. Another unusual locomotive was the ex-Southampton Dock Company '0458' 0-4-0ST, 30458 *'Ironside'*. This diminutive engine acted as the shed pilot for many years. Later, following its withdrawal, it was replaced by a 'B4' of 1891, just a year younger than its predecessor. Yet another LSWR survivor was a 1903 Class 'S11' 4-4-0, 30400, remarkably outlasting the rest of the class by four years until it was condemned in 1955. When mentioning this locomotive in conversation

to my old friend Lew Wooldridge from Guildford, he always enthused about the wonderful paintwork she had when cleaning her even in those very last years. In addition Guildford was host to Drummond 'M7', 'T9' and '700' classes. Some 'Brighton' engines were also to be seen, mainly coming in on Horsham branch services. South Eastern Class 'D' 4-4-0s also regularly worked a number of the Reading to Redhill services. Indeed 31737 is one that survived and can be seen at the National Railway Museum in York in its splendid SE & CR livery.

Back at Feltham we had a number of the Nine Elms-built 'M7' motor tank engines and I recorded firing on Nos 30031, 30032, 30035, 30039, 30043, plus later in 1961/2 30245, 30248, 30051 and 30052. What surprised me even after just a short time at Feltham, was the condition of these M7s, far better than those at Nine Elms, being stronger and steaming well. However it was the footplates that impressed me, for most had burnished copper and brass on the boiler-front that would readily clean beautifully after just a small application of brick dust followed by a rub over with newspaper, No 30043 even showed a great deal of her original scumble painted wood effect on the boiler-front. It was indeed a pleasure to work on a locomotive once this cleaning was complete and in the main it was appreciated by the drivers, who invariably assisted in what I found to be a satisfying exercise. The work these locomotives were employed on was mainly van trains, small freight and empty stock movements to and from various sidings outside the London area. A rather interesting locomotive working was that of 135 and 149 duties that left the shed at 3.52 am. The locomotives involved were an 'M7' coupled to a '700'. Both ran light engine to Twickenham and then double-headed a freight around to Kingston.

FELTHAM DUTY No. 135.
3 F. (700 Class)

—	Feltham Loco. ... ... 3.52 a.m. ‖	
	(coupled to No. 149)	
3.59 a.m.	Twickenham ... ... 4.25 a.m. **F**	
		(A.R.)
4.50 a.m.	Kingston ... ... —	
	F—Shunting 5.0 a.m. to 5.20 a.m.	
—	Kingston ... ... 5.35 a.m. **F**	
5.41 a.m.	Teddington ... ... —	
	F—Shunting 5.45 a.m. to 6.45 a.m.	
—	Teddington ... ... 7. 9 a.m. ‖	
7.29 a.m.	Feltham Loco. ... ...10.46 a.m. ‖	
**	Feltham Yard ... ...11.16 a.m. **F**	
12.56 p.m.	Barnes ... ... —	
	F—Shunting 1.0 p.m. to 2.0 p.m.	
	F—Shunting 2.20 p.m. to 3.30 p.m.	
—	Barnes ... ... 3.32 p.m. ‖	
3.42 p.m.	Kew Bridge ... ... —	
	F—Shunting 3.45 p.m. to 5.15 p.m.	
—	Kew Bridge ... ... 5.15 p.m. ‖	
5.20 p.m.	Chiswick ... ... —	
	F—Shunting 5.20 p.m. to 6.15 p.m.	
—	Chiswick ... ... 6.27 p.m. **F**	
6.50 p.m.	Brentford ... ... —	
	F—Shunting 7.15 p.m. to 7.50 p.m.	
—	Brentford ... ... 7.53 p.m. ‖	
8.10 p.m.	Hounslow New Yard —	
	F—Shunting 8.10 p.m. to 9.20 p.m.	
—	Hounslow ... ... 9.20 p.m. ‖	
9.29 p.m.	Brentford ... ... 9.33 p.m. **F**	
		ANR
9.50 p.m.	Feltham ... ... ** ‖	
**	Feltham Loco. ... ... —	

Feltham Men.

1st set on duty 3,7 a.m., work and relieved 10.46 a.m.

2nd set on duty 10.31 a.m., change to No. 140 at Kew Bridge 4.17 p.m., work and relieved 6.52 p.m.

Off No. 140 change at Kew Bridge 4.17 p.m., work and relieved in depot.

Off No. 79, dispose.

FELTHAM DUTY No. 149.
2 P.T. (M.7 Class)

—	Feltham Loco. ... ... 3.52 a.m. ‖	
	(coupled to No. 135)	
3.59 a.m.	Twickenham ... ... 4.25 a.m. **F**	
5. 5 a.m.	Norbiton ... ... 5.15 a.m. ‖	
5.20 a.m.	Kingston ... ... —	
	F—Shunting 5.20 a.m. to 6.40 a.m.	
	(Less 15 mins. **(M.X.) C** Shunting)	
—	Kingston ... ... 6.45 a.m. ‖	
6.49 a.m.	Norbiton ... ... —	
	F—Shunting 6.50 a.m. to 8.30 a.m.	
—	Norbiton ... ... 8.48 a.m. ‖	
8.53 a.m.	Kingston ... ... —	
	F—Shunting 8.55 a.m. to 2.5 p.m.	
	(Less 30 mins. Meals and E.R.)	
—	Kingston ... ... 2.10 p.m. ‖	
2.33 p.m.	Feltham Loco. ... ... 4.50 p.m. ‖	
4.58 p.m.	Hounslow ... ... 6. 5 p.m. **V**	
	(Via Twickenham)	
6.47 p.m.	Clapham Jc. ... ... 7. 3 p.m. ‖	
7.10 p.m.	Barnes ... ... 7.50 p.m. **F**	

MONDAYS ONLY.

8. 2 p.m.	Brentford ... ... 8.30 p.m. ‖	
8.57 p.m.	Strawberry Hill ... —	
	C.M.E.—Shunting 9.0 p.m. to 9.45 p.m.	
—	Strawberry Hill ... 9.47 p.m. ‖	
10. 0 p.m.	Feltham Loco. ... ... —	

MONDAYS EXCEPTED.

8. 2 p.m.	Brentford ... ... 8.30 p.m. ‖	
8.44 p.m.	Feltham Loco. ... ... —	

Feltham Men.

1st set on duty 3.7 a.m. and relieved Kingston 9.40 a.m. and home passsenger.

2nd set on duty 8.31 a.m., pass. to Kingston relieve 9.40 a.m., work and dispose.

3rd set on duty 4.5 p.m., work and dispose and prepare No. 144.

Here the 'M7' remained for most of the day as the pilot, whilst the '700' performed a pick-up goods duty. Incidentally in those days Kingston signal-box carried the name Kingston Junction for some obscure reason, for there was no junction.

The '700's were known as 'Black Motors', although for reasons unknown. They were also built in 1897 but this time by Dubs & Co of Glasgow. As the reader will probably have deduced by now, they were rather special to me with their open narrow cabs. Somehow they epitomised the engines of their era. If I am allowed a favourite, it would be 30339, and I recorded firing to her on some fifteen occasions. At the end of one particular turn, I recall we brought sister engine No 30689 back to the depot, and my driver Jack Mansey went off into the shed, to return shortly with the Shed Master, Mr Standen who climbed onboard. In our

spare time between shunting, Jack and I had cleaned every part of the footplate, it was a picture with its burnished copper and brass. Mr Standen, himself a keen locomotive man, was extremely complimentary and commented she was good enough for a 'Royal'. Looking back I believe he was quite right! Other '700' engines allocated to Feltham were Nos 30346, 30355, 30687, 30689 and 30696. Some years previous in 1957, another member of the class, 30688, had been involved in a serious accident, when it was struck by an Up Reading train that had started against signals. The resultant collision turned No 30688 onto its side. Due to the damage sustained it was subsequently withdrawn.

As the history of locomotive development shows, the LSWR Urie locomotives were indeed a huge change of direction and improvement from the earlier Adams and Drummond designs. This also became

Class '700' 0-6-0 No 30339 stands briefly on the back road at Feltham just before we went light engine to Twickenham. The diamond shaped Dubs & Co makers plate of 1897 is visible on the middle splasher, as is the oval 70B Feltham shed code plate on the smoke-box door.

apparent to me once I started to regularly work on the four different Urie class locomotives that were still in active service. Despite their antiquity, they still performed admirably at the head of heavy freight trains and my log book of those times has provided invaluable recordings of all the work I performed on them at Feltham.

None of the original 1914 built 'H15', 4-6-0 locomotives, 'Tavys' as they were known, nor the subsequent 1924 members of the class, were allocated to Feltham during my time. Although a few years earlier in

1950, both Nos 30330 and 30331 were allocated to the depot. In 1960 however they would still come on shed occasionally and as such I fired on 30489 on a freight train to Basingstoke in August 1960 and again in November, this time on the 'two trips' turn to Nine Elms Goods from Feltham Yard.

On both occasions I noted the engine was in good condition. Just a year later, in 1961, the same could not be said for 30521, which I recorded as being in rather poor condition when working the same duty. Other locomotives in the class that I fired on were

'G16' 4-8-0T No 30495 looking as immaculate as a freight engine can. Seen here recently out of the works with her new paint and British Railways emblem on the sloping side tanks. These extremely powerful locomotives were regularly used on the Willesden, Neasden and Brent (Cricklewood) interchange freight services.

'H16' 4-6-2T, No 30519, stands in Reading South shed after being turned and watered for the return working to Feltham Yard. In the distant background a Class 'V', 4-4-0, is reversing towards Reading General in readiness for the Birkenhead to Dover working, known as the 'Continental'.

30482, 30484, 30486, 30522, 30523, 30524 and 30491, unfortunately at that time sadly coming to the end of their days.

The 'G16' 4-8-0T locomotives of 1921/22 were specifically built for the new Feltham marshalling yard that incorporated two hump-shunting facilities in both the Up and Down direction. They were based on the 'S15' but with smaller boilers similar to the 'D15' 4-4-0 locomotives. They were fitted with both steam-operated brakes and reverser, extremely helpful when shunting. The combination of small-coupled wheels and large cylinders gave them the highest LSWR locomotive tractive effort recorded. Interestingly they were at first allocated to Strawberry Hill prior to the depot at Feltham being opened.

Whilst I had observed all four of the 'G16's during the fifties, by the time I arrived at Feltham in the spring of 1960 both 30492 and sister engine 30493 had been withdrawn in 1959. Steam operation on the hump shunting turns had also ceased from 1954 following the introduction of the original Derby-built diesel shunting locomotives 13040-2. However 30494 and 30495 were still gainfully employed in early 1960. My records actually show the same amount of footplate work, collectively some thirty-four turns in all, on both of

these leviathan tank locomotives.

The 'H16' 4-6-2T locomotives, 'Green Tanks' as they were known, appeared to be similar in many ways, but were in fact very different. Their larger 5' 7" diameter driving wheels and of course the 4-6-2 wheel arrangement made them quite a free running locomotive. Probably the only limiting factor as regards their availability was water capacity and this needed to be checked regularly. They were used on interchange freight service with the other regions as well as working in and about both Nine Elms Goods and Wimbledon Yards. I recorded over sixty turns of duty on these locomotives. Rarely did they venture too far afield, however I can recall they regularly were seen on Guildford shed.

One exception to their normally limited area of operation was on Saturday 16th July 1960, when the customary 'S15' locomotive was not available for a morning Reading freight turn, 115 duty. Thus 30519 deputised as the replacement engine. Ensuring that the side tanks were full of water and with plenty of coal in the bunker during preparation we made a good start to the day's work ahead. Needless to say the locomotive was more than adequate for both legs of the turn. We turned the loco in Reading depot, 70E, for our return

The precursor of the 1920 'Urie' built S15 4-6-0s No. 30496 stands at Ascot in 1960 with the 6.10am Feltham Yard to Reading freight. We were waiting for an early morning Waterloo to Reading and Guildford service to pass. The station's Southern Railway's 'Odeon' style signal box is the back-ground. This was one of the four boxes that operated the Ascot area in mechanical days. Driver Reggie Masterson is seen in the photograph whilst the customary can of tea stands on top of the vacuum ejector keeping warm.

journey and fortunately I was able to take the accompanying photograph on the day.

So far as Feltham was concerned, in my opinion it was the Urie 'S15s' which formed the backbone of the depot. They were indeed the 'main line' engines of 70B shed, versatile, reliable and powerful. The type were to be seen in numerous locations on the South Western section whilst overall I recorded more than one hundred firing turns on these splendid locomotives. In Southern Region days they carried the numbers 30496 - 30515 and were maintained by Feltham virtually all this time.

In the summer time, particularly on Saturdays, Feltham crews would work them to Salisbury and return with the additional holiday passenger traffic from the West of England.

It was no mean feat to get a 'Goods Engine' to perform along the same lines as a *bona fide* 'Passenger Engine' and despite some of the barbed comments of the Nine Elms crews they didn't do that bad really. There always was a degree of superiority shown by the Nine Elms enginemen whenever Feltham men were to be seen

on the main line on such occasions.

Having been involved in both heavy freight working and fast passenger work, the driving skills required are obviously very different. It was indeed a pleasure to work with drivers that had the expertise to cater with both types of trains using the precision demanded. Fortunately I suffered few experiences of poor locomotive driving; however there were some that made hard work of it, they shall remain nameless.

On one occasion I remember preparing an 'S15' for a Feltham Yard to Reading freight when Inspector George Bolland climbed up on to the footplate. He indicated to the driver that he was riding with us to observe the locomotive's performance and whilst doing so wanted to carry out some tests. Apparently the engine had been booked for poor steaming, but following examination nothing had been found to be the likely cause. "Forewarned is Forearmed" so to speak, hence I took great care in the preparation of the fire.

Getting away from Feltham westbound, was easy going with the gradient in our favour. This was

Reading (Southern) Yard. A 1960 view from the footplate of 'H16' 30519, with the Southern's terminus station in the distance on the left and centrally, the locomotive depot. The lower quadrant signals of the Western Region can be seen in the background.

followed by a slight pull over the Thames at Staines bridge then down through Egham, whereupon the heavy work starts with the regulator firmly in the second valve. By now also the fire was extremely hot and the engine was responding to the short rounds of firing, however it was soon clear that the boiler would not maintain steam pressure with the injector continuously working, even cut fine. Inspector Bolland examined the fire himself several times but made no comment. In these circumstances it is a balance between the boiler's water level and steam pressure and by letting the water level drop you can preserve the steam pressure, which is exactly what I did. Also knowing the road and equally what your driver will do at certain points en route is important. In the meantime, Inspector Bolland was emptying sachets of coloured powder into the fire-box and then immediately observing the chimney and taking notes. Ascot was duly passed with half a glass of water and only about 150lbs pressure; then with the regulator eased we slowly regained the lost water and steam. We continued on to Reading Yard with no problem as the demand on the boiler was by now not so great. Whatever happened to the locomotive in the aftermath of this test I never did find out!

Later, when I was at Nine Elms in 1963, another memorable incident occurred early one morning when working an up freight from Salisbury to Nine Elms with a Feltham Urie-built 'S15'. After being relieved in the platform off our down working, we were in turn booked to relieve Salisbury men in the Up Yard about 3.00 am. At this time Bill Turner was my regular driver in what was No 2 link, known as the 'Pilot Gang'. So, after making the requisite can of tea, we made our way, in the dark, to the far end of the yard. Relieving the

crew, we were told the engine was in good order. I checked the head-lamps and made some final preparation to the fire and then ensured the back damper was fully open before we were signalled away. Approaching Salisbury Tunnel, I exchanged hand-signals with the Guard and all was well. After passing Laverstock Intermediate Block signal we started climbing the bank up to Porton, the engine steaming freely and the train following along nicely. The first hint of a problem emerged some 30-odd miles later as we passed Worting Junction and approached Winklebury intermediate signals. Now with the regulator closed and the engine coasting, a rather heavy knock was evident, so much so that Bill lightly applied steam whilst still braking the train in order to cushion whatever was causing the effect. As we entered the yard at Basingstoke something else caused further concern, the pungent smell of hot oil and metal. Once stationary, Bill climbed down and immediately examined the locomotive. He quickly determined one of the driving-wheel axle-boxes was severely over-heated. On returning to the footplate he checked the oil levels in the brass oil boxes that provided lubrication to the axles. The trimmings were all correctly in place and the oil levels appeared to be more than sufficient. However closer examination revealed that some of the boxes were actually full of water, with a thin layer of oil floating on the top. Needless to say this was the cause of the problem and we both set about removing the offending water.

Bill then 'dosed' up the axle-box in question by removing the trimming and filling the oil box with warm thick oil, normally used in the hydrostatic lubricator. This rapidly found its way down to the axle-box, via the copper pipe that linked it to the oil-box. Bill decided that we would continue to Woking our next stop where he would consider the condition of the locomotive. As it was, we eventually continued all the way through to Nine Elms Goods with Bill nursing the ailing engine, along with careful use of the regulator and brake, plus constant applications of thick oil en-route. Later I saw the locomotive under the hoist at Nine Elms, the driving wheels out and the axle-box requiring urgent re-metalling. The reason for the water in the oil-boxes could have been that the boiler had been washed out, most unusually, at Salisbury. Water spillage from the wash out plugs in the boiler backhead, used for cleaning scale off the top of the fire-box, may have caused the problem. Obviously this should not have occurred as it was part of the boiler maintenance program to ensure that the oil boxes were not contaminated with water after a wash out was completed.

Life in Feltham No 3 link continued and I recorded my first trip to Hither Green, firing to John Mason on 'Q1' 33027. The mileage between the two yards isn't great, however it is an extremely interesting line to work over with a loose-coupled train. In particular, the gradients between Clapham Junction and Hither Green are quite severe and require a great degree of skill on the part of the driver. The changes in the gradient over a short distance also demanded that the vehicle couplings were kept taut in order to avoid 'snatching' that could cause a coupling to break followed by all the ensuing problems that this created. The guard at the rear of the train could also be injured in the event of a heavy snatch occurring.

Naturally, running with stretched couplings could only be achieved when under clear signals, whereas when signals indicated caution, the train required to be buffered-up, in order that the full weight was against the locomotive, so the brakes could be applied to the degree required.

Working freight trains was indeed a team effort, for the guard played a major part in slowing the train from the van at the rear. On a falling gradient the guard's application of his handbrake would be felt on the footplate, as all the couplings became taut as the train stretched out between the van and the engine. It was a pleasure to watch a good freight driver and guard working so well together; speed was not the essence of the exercise, it was timing and skill.

Starting a freight train, and picking it up again after running under caution signals, was a delicate balance of easing the locomotive away from the train without excessive snatches. If you consider for one moment that the amount of movement there is between each wagon from when the coupling is taut to when the buffers are in contact, is roughly nine inches; now multiply that by sixty, an average freight train length,

and you have the total movement from the front of a buffered-up stationary train before the rear of the train ever begins to move, in this scenario is five hundred and forty inches, some fifteen yards.

The year 1960 witnessed my first trip over the route to Hither Green. As we approached Lewisham I saw the temporary girder bridge that crossed the main line from Charing Cross and Cannon Street near St Johns, still showing signs of the urgent repairs made in the aftermath of the tragic disaster of that occurred there some three years earlier. I well recall the press coverage of that fateful evening involving 'Battle of Britain' 34066 'Spitfire'.

A 'Q1' was in fact the ideal locomotive on the Hither Green route, with its high boiler pressure of 220lbs, good adhesion and immense power. If one was not available, a '700' would be the usual alternative, although on such occasions working the service would demand a different approach. The smaller boiler and lower pressure of 175lbs alone meant the locomotive was worked to its maximum in places.

It was not unusual to observe Eastern Region 'J69' 0-6-0Ts and London Midland '8F' 2-8-0s, or even an occasional 'WD' 2-8-0, from either Hornsey or Willesden, in both the Hither Green and Feltham areas. These arrived on the inter-regional freights. What I do remember when passing close by, was their individual and distinct 'regional' smell. It really was somewhat bizarre that you could instantly recognise a 'foreigner' by your nose, even if couldn't actually see them to identify the exact class of locomotive. Sometimes when returning from annual leave you would briefly catch your own distinct Southern smell, unfortunately it never lasted very long!

Another interesting route that became more familiar during my time at Feltham, was that to Temple Mills Yard on the Eastern Region. Located near the former GER 'gargantuan' depot of Stratford, 30A, in North East London, it was indeed an event to work freight trains in and out of this matrix of railways. The varieties of routes that could be presented to the Southern locomotive crews required a great degree of vigilance by enginemen when approaching and working in and out of the yard. On several occasions Stratford-based crews would come up to one of our locomotives in the yard and ask to come on the footplate. They clearly were impressed with performance of our locomotives when seen in action and couldn't understand how such relatively small machines handled with ease such heavy loads.

On one occasion as we came off our train and took the usual avoiding line around the hump at Temple Mills we were treated to a spectacle the yard supervisor would rather not have occurred. Instead of a wagon coming off the hump and being slowed by the 'primary'

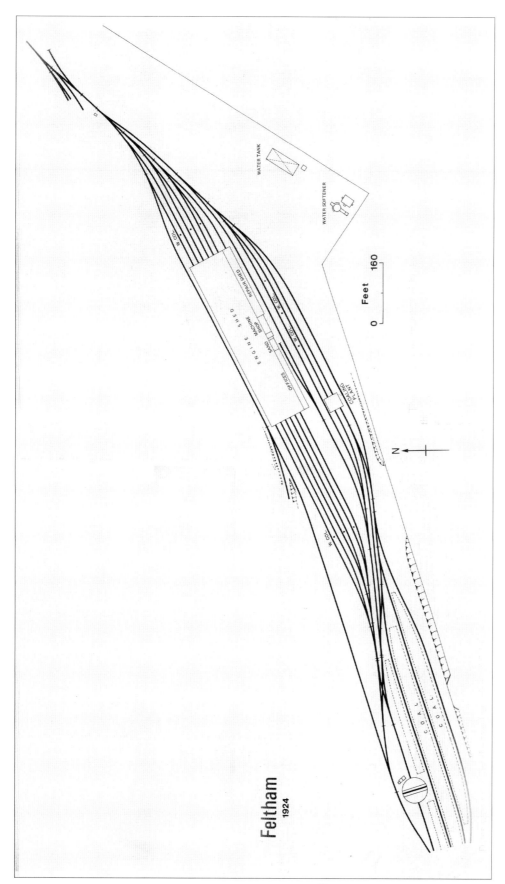

Feltham 1924
Feltham 1924. The marshalling yard was situated to north of the depot. The 'Khyber' siding is not shown.

Taken from 'An Historical Survey of Southern Sheds' Chris Hawkins and George Reeve. Ian Allan / OPC.

London and South Western Ry. 787
TO
WINDSOR & ETON

retarder, it evidently missed this completely and was heading towards a line of stationary stock at some speed. The 'secondary' retarder, was activated somewhat enthusiastically, from the control box, as when the wagon reached it, it did not just slow, but stood it on end, on to its buffers to be more accurate. We left them to clear up the mess.

Whilst I'm sure much has been written of the former GER Stratford Works, the Depot and of all the men who worked there, none is more eminent than that of Richard Hardy's wonderfully descriptive series of articles, 'Stratford Forever'. They remind us all of those times, good, bad and indifferent, that will never be seen and perhaps never heard of again. We are indeed privileged to share such vivid memories.

The route to Brent Sidings on the old Midland Railway passed by several of the older London motive power depots, the GWR's Old Oak Common, 81A, the LNWR's Willesden, 1A, the GCR's Neasden, 34E, and the Midland's freight depot at Cricklewood, 14A. There was also plenty to see during a trip in that direction, from 'Kings', 'Castles' and 'Halls' to 'Black Fives', 'Royal Scots', '8Fs', then 'A3s', 'B1s', 'V2s' and finally '9Fs' and more '8Fs'. It really was a panorama of steam still active and vibrant in the early sixties. Occasionally, especially in bad weather conditions and when working a tender engine, we would drop back into Cricklewood to turn, either in the round-house or on the loop, especially installed for turning the Beyer Garrett locomotives.

One particularly bad day was 26th June 1961. We had a train for Brent sidings with 33038, when we slipped to a standstill on the heavy gradient, just under the bridge at the back of the Cricklewood depot. This was a notorious location, where incidentally, pigeon droppings on the railhead may well have been a contributing factor to the poor adhesion, hence there was a suitable engineman's nickname for the offending bridge. We had to request assistance and eventually a reasonably new diesel locomotive came to our aid, in the shape of a 'Peak' No D9, 'Snowdon'.

It was during the period that I worked the transfer freight trains that a somewhat sinister turn of events occurred at Cricklewood depot. The first of these concerned a '9F', 2-10-0. At the start this was rung out of the depot as per the usual practice, the working being stated as 'light engine to Wellingborough'. The signalman responded to the information provided by means of the telephone located at the depot exit signal and duly set the route. The locomotive departed in the customary fashion and nothing at all unusual was noted as it continued on its way, displaying the correct lamps to front and rear. No doubt the quadrupled track on the Midland mainline provided a clear route for the movement, as undoubtedly something far more serious

might have occurred if the circumstances had been different. Sometime later the engine came to a standstill more than ten miles down the line, having run out of steam and water. Someone locally was eventually dispatched to investigate what was a long delay, but on arrival it was found to be crewless, completely unmanned.

There were other instances of malevolent intent. Indeed on one particular evening just before Christmas, it involved one of our Southern crews and their locomotive. As mentioned previously, the 'H16', 4-6-2Ts were regularly used on the regional transfer freights and whilst one of them, 30520, was pulling its train out from the sidings, a serious collision occurred with another locomotive. The force of this was such as to turn the H16 onto it side. The Feltham crew were extremely fortunate to escape uninjured in the circumstances. In the aftermath, it was surprising that neither the driver, Bill Feaver nor his fireman, Brian Alderton, were ever summonsed to any formal inquiry, despite the fact that the other engine involved was again found to be unmanned. Naturally the British Transport Police were actively involved for sometime, as clearly someone with a both good knowledge of railways and the procedures and movements associated with Cricklewood depot was suspected, perhaps an ex-employee with a grievance. We never did hear whether anyone was eventually apprehended but we were certainly more than wary when working in the area following the incident.

Working trains under the Absolute Block Signalling regulations that existed on the inter-regional routes previously described, was certainly difficult on occasions. Weather conditions in October and November were always very bad, the autumn leaf fall period caused slipping and even worse when the locomotives would 'pick-up' their wheels under braking. This was followed by the perennial November fogs that lasted well into December. The need for efficient working sand apparatus and full sand-boxes on the locomotive was absolutely essential and drivers would take great care to ensure that everything was in order before coming off the shed.

From the fireman's point of view this demanded the laborious task of carrying numerous, extremely heavy, sand hoppers from the sand storage point to the locomotive, then lifting them up onto the running plate before empting the contents into the boxes. I'm sure my arms were somewhat longer after a session of this activity, that incidentally was only deemed satisfactorily completed when the sandboxes were brimming full. On the other hand fog was not so much a physical issue as more a mental one. A matter of concentration, engine management and good route knowledge. Fog-signalmen would be dispatched to place detonators on the rails at the distant signals and so warn footplate crews of the signal's position. During thick fog we might also have Double-Block working introduced, that would almost bring the railway to standstill. This method of regulating ensured there was always a clear block section between the successive trains. Thereby in the event that a train in the rear inadvertently passed signals at Danger, it would not immediately collide with the rear of the stationary train in front. Naturally marshalling yards became completely blocked by the lack of movement that then resulted. Trains standing at signals on the running lines, sometimes for hours at a time. It was painfully slow proceeding through the fog searching for the next Stop signal, having to check ones progress by bridges and close line-side features that had been memorised over the years. On some tall semaphore signals, the post or gantry was, on occasions, viewed first in the fog and confirmation of the signals position when stationary sometimes required closer inspection from the ground, or even up the signal ladder in severe conditions. Many times I have then had to walk through the eerily quiet fog to a signal-box to sign the Train-Register and carry out 'Rule 55'. This regulation acted as a reminder to the Signalman that he had a train standing at his signals, even though he couldn't see it most of the time. Track-circuits and telephones later provided an invaluable aid to overcome this situation, however the rule still had to be applied in most cases for many years even after these improvements. In addition one must also remember that at that time, the introduction of the 'Automatic Warning System' was still very much in its infancy and only gave an indication of the distant signal's position in semaphore signalled areas.

Sadly some of the 'H16, 4-6-2T's were transferred from Feltham to Eastleigh depot in the early sixties and thereafter used on tank-car traffic over the Fawley branch from Totton in Hampshire. In actual fact they were not particularly successful on the route and eventually returned to Feltham to end their days. During the period that they were 70B allocated I recorded over sixty firing turns overall, embracing all the five members of the class whilst I was at Feltham. In turn, as replacements for the transferred locomotives, Feltham received some 'W' 2-6-4T locomotives, made redundant due to both electrification and dieselisation of the South East and Central sections of the Southern Region. They were ten years younger than the somewhat aged 'H16's, having been built in Southern Railway days in 1931. These Maunsell locomotives were indeed extremely different in their concept, Belpaire fireboxes, taper boilers and three cylinders, they were also the last British built class of locomotive to have brakes fitted to their bogies, provided in order to improve the locomotive's brake force. The footplate area was quite

comfortable to work in and the cab design certainly protected the crews from the vagaries of the weather. Clearly some of the features of the somewhat maligned, and subsequently scrapped, 'K' tank locomotives of 1927 had survived and were duly incorporated within their design. On a practical note they rode extremely well at speed, as I recall when working vans and empty stock and more importantly they could equally, indeed more than adequately, handle any of our transfer freight turns. I duly recorded over twenty firing turns on four of the class whilst at Feltham, this included working on, 31912, 31916, 31923 and 31924 between 1960 and 1962. As might be expected, they were in many ways similar to the 'U', 'N', 'U1' and 'N1' classes in terms of their boiler and general layout, and in my opinion were splendid engines. The only negative aspect of a 'W' being that the inside cylinder required the driver to climb underneath to oil the various parts of the associated inside motion.

In the early 1960's Feltham saw some changes in respect to the South Western locomotive classes that were normally to be seen on shed. For some months there were a number of suitability 'tests' that took place with engines like a 'Brighton' Class 'K', 2-6-0, Class WD, 2-8-0, and Class 'Q', 0-6-0, unfortunately none of which I had the opportunity of working upon. How they were actually assessed I never discovered but nothing positive ever came from the exercise. Whilst BR 'Standard' class locomotives were allocated to many other Southern Region depots none of the various classes were officially allocated at Feltham, nor performed any of the depot's designated duties up until the time I returned to Nine Elms.

Like the Standard classes, none of the 'U' or 'N' 2-6-0's, were ever allocated to Feltham during my time, although I did work on them occasionally. At that time in store on the 'Khyber' siding, located at the East end of the shed, were four 'D1' 4-4-0's, 31494, 31727, 31545 and 31246. All had sacking over their chimneys and were destined never to work again. I took the opportunity of climbing on each; it was a melancholy experience.

Whilst these particular engines would never be steamed again, there were other classes that continued in service and I recorded turns on the 3-cylinder 'U1's, 31892/3/5/6, and on 'Ls' 31753/60. On one turn '118 and 80' duty, we signed on at 10.12 pm and would work a freight at 10.45 pm from Feltham West End, via Chertsey, to Wimbledon Yard with a 'Q1', calling at Walton and dropping off a number of wagons before continuing. After shunting the yard at Wimbledon we would run light-engine to Clapham Junction and get relief. Thereafter we would walk to Nine Elms and prepare our engine to work a van train to Feltham from Waterloo at 4.40 am, calling at Kew Bridge, Brentford and Hounslow. We had 'U1' No 31909 on this working for a couple of days but then rather specially for the next three days, a 'Glasshouse' 'L1', No. 31786. With its 6' 8" driving wheels, this was a true main line engine. On the last day of the turn the normal Guildford relief crew at Feltham were delayed and I was asked to work the end part of the turn. This then proceeded to call at Staines, Ascot, Camberley and then Woking, via Frimley Junction and Sturt Lane Junction. After shunting the train in the yard we ran light-engine to Guildford depot from Woking Yard. What a wonderful locomotive to work on, although then coming to the end of its working life it was a savoured pleasure to be on the footplate of an engine dating back to 1926. It was withdrawn nine months later in February 1962.

Unusually on the 15th August 1961, I was booked on a weed-killer train within Feltham Yard. My driver was Bill Kench and our booked locomotive, 'U1' No 31896. Following preparation we made our way to the yard, coupled on to the train and then began a slow speed traverse of both the 'arrival' and 'departure' roads whilst spraying. All these movements were under the supervision of a senior shunter, as the yard was fully operational at the time. During a period that we were stationary waiting for access to yet another road, I heard someone calling out, 'Help, help, I'm under the engine'. Immediately I climbed down from to examine the underside. There was no one there nor nearby in the adjacent roads. Returning to the footplate Bill asked me where I had been, so I explained what had happened. 'Well I never heard anything', he said. Still waiting to move, I again heard further cries for help and looked across the footplate at Bill. It then dawned on me what he was doing as he laughed about the episode. He was in fact a very good ventriloquist I learned later, and I was just another one of his victims. However there is more, for after completing all the movements required in the yard we then ran light engine to the depot, where we stopped with the locomotive under the coal hopper ready to top up the tender. Suddenly Joe, the African coal-hopper man, came flying out of his small cabin looking absolutely terrified and ran up the shed, shouting. Eventually the Running Foreman came to the locomotive and had stern words with Bill about what he had done. Clearly he had thrown his voice into the cabin. This had frightened poor Joe, who firmly believed in superstition that Bill was a 'Voodoo man'. We never did get any coal that day whilst it took ages to get Joe calmed down and back to work.

Earlier in 1959, along with my friend Alan Wilton, I travelled down to Ashford to have a tour of the works. Even then there were indications that closure would not be too far in the future. Despite this ominous fact, the works was still quite active with numerous classes of locomotives to be seen in and outside. Class

'V', Nos 30932/33/39, 'L1', No 31759, 'E1', No 31019, 'U1' No 31891, 'N1', 'No 31880, 'E4' No 32578, 'C2X, No 32516, 'N', Nos 31408, 31814/16/18/35/44/51, 'H', 31322, 31500/12/17/33, 'C', Nos 31693 /94, 'U', Nos 31612/24, 31803, 'Q1', Nos 33016/22/29/30.

'N' class 2-6-0, No. 31858 was noted standing outside the works in an extremely run-down rusty condition, however on entering the shops a duplicate locomotive, also No 31858, was immaculately presented and ready to leave. Interestingly the works staff assured us that this locomotive had been built from all new and existing spares in the works, frames, boiler, fittings and in their opinion represented the last steam locomotive ever built on the Southern. Two years later, on 17th February 1961 I recorded my one and only trip on No. 31858, working a freight from Woking Yard to Feltham Yard, in the remarks column I had noted 'Exceptionally good locomotive'!

In those days, most stations in the Feltham area still had thriving goods yards and there were a number of pick-up goods turns that supplied the various commodities of the day not yet delivered by long distance lorries and vans. Coal for household use would be deliver by the wagon load, some local merchants, still having horse-drawn vehicles. If we had perishables on board, these would normally be placed in the local goods shed for unloading in dry conditions. Other produce, perhaps seasonal, would be either in vans or under tarpaulin-clad wagons. Some businesses also had their own sidings for steel and timber delivery. It was this situation, replicated at almost every station up and down the line, that provided the requirement for Feltham depot and its variety of allocated locomotives.

One of these local turns, was the 'Windsor Goods', which ran from Feltham yard early every morning and before the electric commuter service started. Normally a '700', was the designated locomotive, however I did record an 'N' on several occasions. Sometimes we would run non-stop to Windsor and after crossing 'Black Potts' bridge, would be signalled directly into the yard, situated at the side of the River Thames. Shunting would not normally commence until about 7.00 am so there was plenty of time in hand. We had thus to keep the engine quiet or we would be in trouble. This was done by damping-down the fire with small coal, no emissions of excessive steam or smoke was the order of the day. In the summer months I would often take a walk around during the intervening period. On one such occasion I found another steam powered vehicle close by in the form of a large pleasure riverboat belonging to 'Salter's Steamers'. This was moored immediately alongside their landing stage, very near to Windsor & Eton Riverside station. Although ageing, the boat was in

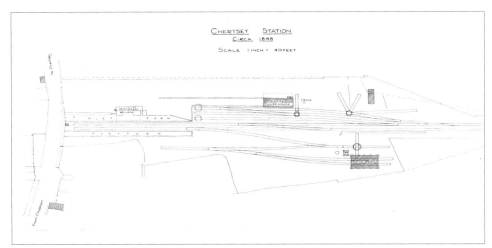

Chertsey, circa 1848.

beautifully condition with a white hull and funnel, appropriately named "Queen of the Thames". Whilst I stood there admiring the vessel a hatch opened and the boat's elderly engineer popped his head out. We had a chat about steam in general and I was invited to come onboard and examine the marine type boiler, valve-gear and the drive arrangement, all of it of course highly polished.

Following electrification of the line, Windsor's two-road locomotive shed had closed in the mid-1930s, but was still extant in 1960 and in relatively good condition. It was then being used by the local coal merchant to garage his lorries. The small, disused internal lobby, with its notice board and pigeon-holes for the crews, plus the oil store were all still to be seen. Jim Robinson senior, originally an old Feltham engineman, told me a number of stories about the shed dating back to LSWR days. In those days, a small gang of cleaners would regularly travel from Feltham down to Windsor on the last train and clean the resident 'M7s'. After cleaning was completed they would sometimes 'borrow' a punt and paddle off up the river and get up to all manner of things.

The Southern, like the other railway companies, had developed their distinct corporate identity in respect to the manner they painted their station buildings which including signal-boxes, green, yellow and white being the principal colours used. After nationalisation the Southern Region had continued in a similar way, except, that is, for the signal-box at Windsor, which was painted all green to blend in with the surrounding foliage and so not be seen from the castle! When making the tea one morning, the signalman amusingly told me that, having washed out some dusters, he had hung them out to dry just outside the box, only to receive stern instruction from the station to remove them immediately as someone from the castle had complained and had phoned down to the Station Master. I have often wondered *who* it actually was who had complained.

Chertsey, like Windsor & Eton Riverside, still had its old locomotive shed intact, despite having closing in 1936. The original early branch line was built in 1848 from Weybridge to a terminus at Chertsey. In those days the station was located on the Weybridge side of the present day level crossing. Later, when the line was extended to Virginia Water in 1866, another station to the west of the original was built to accommodate through trains linking up with the new Reading line.

The branch line from Weybridge to Virginia Water was normally worked by a 'Push & Pull' service thereby alleviating running round at either end of the short journey. However, when a motor-fitted locomotive was not available for the service, running-round would become an un-welcomed additional duty for the crews involved.

There were actually three other depots operating in the Feltham area up until the mid-thirties, in addition to those at Windsor and Chertsey. The other was at Ascot, where a single road shed was located next to the curve that went off to Bagshot and Camberley, 'M7' No 126, the only superheated locomotive of the class being allocated there for a period. Alf Hurley, my last driver in the top-link at Nine Elms, told me he fired to her a number of times in Southern Railway days. Oddly there was a small turntable at Ascot during that time. It was to be found in the Up Yard between the goods shed and the station. Just how often it was used I'm not altogether sure, but I certainly turned a locomotive on it on more than one occasion, either a '700' or a 'Q1'. Further up the line at Virginia Water, the triangular junction allowed trains from Chertsey to directly gain access to the Reading line, extremely handy when operating difficulties occurred. One particular pick-up goods turn, '125' duty, used the connection, known as the West Curve, continuing on to sometimes shunt the Government sidings at Longcross, Sunningdale and then Ascot yards. Later we would return to Feltham, shunting sometimes at both 'Drake &

Mounts' siding at the top of the bank at Sunninghill and then Virginia Water. All these local stations mentioned were regularly visited by the pick-up goods trains of the day that were either crewed by Feltham, Guildford or Reading depot's enginemen

In March 1961 promotion came into No.2 link but which also brought to a close my working with Derek Leming. My new driver was Alf Greenaway, a somewhat older, more staid man who had quite a different personality from Derek. For the first few days together very little was said across the footplate and I soon learned that he was a thoughtful man by nature. There was nothing meant by this manner and I became accustomed to both his demeanour and his method of working. I recall the occasion when we were taking water at Neasden with a 'G16'. Without warning the water column pipe buckled under pressure and came out of the filling point, immediately sending water cascading down the side tank, absolutely drenching him. Without a word he calmly turned off the water valve,

SOUTHERN REGION
Feltham Motive Power Depot Circa 1960
Locomotive 'DOWN' Departure Times

Duty	Time	Destination	Comments
102	12.37 am	Southampton	
157	1.50 am	Twickenham	
103	3.49 am	Eastleigh	
113	4.12 am	Reading	
134	4.27 am	Windsor & Eton	
146	5.20 am	Clapham Yard	
151	5.25 am	West End	
125	5.52 am	Reading	
135	6.22 am	Egham	Light engine
112	6.23 am	Weybridge	
150	6.27 am	Station Pilot	
152	8.00 am	Loco shunter	Light engine
117	8.40 am	Reading	Light engine
121	9.00 am	Guildford	
105	9.27 am	Eastleigh	
120	10.56 am	Reading	
123	11.27 am	Woking	
134	1.10 pm	Weybridge	Light engine
143	1.56 pm	Surbiton	
125	2.23 pm	Woking	Light engine
107	2.27 pm	Southampton	
126	7.26 pm	Reading	
110	7.57 pm	Woking	
186	8.57 pm	Guildford	
125	10.27 pm	Wimbledon	
102	10.56 pm	Eastleigh	
108	11.35 pm	Salisbury	
124	11.40 pm	Woking	
146	11.57 pm	Wimbledon	

SOUTHERN REGION
Feltham Motive Power Depot Circa 1960
Locomotive 'Up' Departure Times

Duty	Time	Destination	Comments
122	12.19 am	Nine Elms	
67	12.30 am	Nine Elms	
139	1.34 am	Willesden	
113	3.45 am	Nine Elms	
133	3.52 am	Twickenham	Coupled light engines
149	3.52 am	Twickenham	Coupled light engines
140	5.20 am	Willesden	
132	5.30 am	Twickenham	Light engine
123	6.24 am	Brent	
126	7.21 am	Neasden	
124	8.24 am	Brent	
128	8.43 am	Temple Mills	
69	10.00 am	Nine Elms	
122	10.27 am	Nine Elms	
139	12.15 pm	Willesden	
113	1.22 pm	Nine Elms	
124	1.47 am	Hither Green	
133	2.04 pm	Twickenham	Light engine
122	4.27 pm	Neasden	
149	4.50 pm	Hounslow	Light engine
128	5.58 pm	Temple Mills	
146	6.27 pm	Brent	
108	6.45 pm	Willesden	
140	7.25 pm	Neasden	
470	7.43 pm	Hounslow	Light engine
109	8.45 pm	Nine Elms	
104	9.55 pm	Hither Green	
139	10.15 pm	Willesden	
120	10.47 pm	Hither Green	
121	11.50 pm	Temple Mills	

asked if we had enough water and climbed back on to the footplate where he removed his coat and attempted to dry himself. Naturally I apologised, feeling somewhat guilty, but he would hear nothing of it, he regarding it as just one of those things. At the end of our first week together, we were standing coupled to our train in Willesden South West sidings, waiting for the tip to start. He came over the footplate and quietly asked if I would like to drive back to Feltham. This was my first opportunity to drive over the route and I always considered it a privilege throughout my firing career to be offered a drive. Still only 18, I always believed the golden rule was to drive any locomotive exactly the same as your driver did. Once we were on our way the initial trepidation soon faded and I began to enjoy the experience of handling a heavy train on the demanding falling gradient down towards Kew and then the onward climb to Feltham Yard. I realised from that moment that I was appreciated and trusted by him, thereupon a close working relationship was formed. It was indeed a pleasure to be his fireman during this period and I cherish the times that we shared together.

In order to give some idea of the day-to-day departures of locomotives from Feltham depot I have copied, from the records in my notebook of 1960, the various destinations of engines throughout a twenty-four period, these are shown on pages 33 and 34. Nothing quite like the movements at Nine Elms but interesting nevertheless considering the yard destinations involved now long gone.

Another change took place in August 1961 as Alf Greenaway moved into the Top Link and my next regular driver became Tom Oxenham. He was a likeable old chap, although his worrying disposition did not provide the best of working relationships.

Unfortunately I can recall two incidents where we over-ran signals, both at junctions, luckily without any great cause for concern. The first was at Addlestone Junction with No 33027 in August and then at Feltham Junction on No 31924 in September. On both occasions I had to act rapidly, by getting to the box to report the situation and wait for instructions. Surprisingly enough, to my knowledge, nothing ever came of these indiscretions, however I certainly never had the same amount of confidence in him that I had with my previous drivers. Much of the firing work that I recorded at this time was on a variety of 'Q1s', a number of which that had been transferred in from the Eastern section. No 33040 in particular was noted as being in poor condition, valve gear, bearings, etc.

Rather unusually on the 25th August 1961, I recorded working an early morning special from Feltham Yard to Hither Green, '73C', with an original Bulleid pacific, 'WC' No 34094 'Mortehoe'. This was an old Nine Elms locomotive that I had previously cleaned and fired on a number of occasions. After turning at Hither Green, we took the engine back light (home) to Nine Elms.

Oddly enough on the 27th September 1961, I recorded that 'H16' No 30516 had been modified after many years of service. The water feed valve control was normally operated by the foot, located on the footplate floor near to the cab door. However, a simple extension had now been added and the water valve was now manually operated. What Mr. Urie would have said I can't imagine!

The period firing to Tom Oxenham was indeed a short one for now it was my turn to move and I was promoted into the top link in early October, this time with Albert Soundy, one of Feltham's more senior drivers. What a pleasure the next months were to be working with him, an absolute gentleman. As with most depots the top link's work content recognised the seniority of the drivers, although certainly not the firemen for sure. Even so much of the preparation & disposal work was now left to others as the majority of the turns we took were 'runners'.

I have also recorded some events unusual for the time. One rare occasion saw 'LN' No 30857 'Lord Howe' on Feltham shed which we then prepared and used to run some vans down to Twickenham on the 13th December 1961 A few days later on the 19th December, we worked twenty vans down to Woking from Waterloo with 'V' No 30902 'Wellington', the only time that I ever worked on a 'Schools' whilst at Feltham. Again required to work at Nine Elms we prepared 'E4' No 32487 and took empty stock in and out of Waterloo, I recorded that the loco was in good condition. Yet another pacific worked on whilst on shed at Feltham depot was 'WC' No 34017 'Ilfracombe'.

A rather grubby Class 'V', 4-4-0, No 30902 'Wellington' coupled to Standard Class '4' 2-6-0 wait to drop back into the depot following their arrival at Redhill. Loco hauled through trains reversed before continuing onwards to Tonbridge or Reading.

The design of larger mainline locomotives made the old 1876-built Nine Elms roundhouse depot unable to cope with such motive power developments. As such the emergence of a huge fifteen-road running shed, served by a larger fifty-foot turntable, took place in 1885, and a further increase in size occurred later in 1889. In 1910 another ten road section was added alongside the existing 'Old Shed', this became known as the 'New Shed', thus providing a twenty-five road depot. The large adjacent roundhouse depot of 1876, like its predecessors, was eventually abandoned and demolished years later.

The old and the new at Nine Elms. In LSWR days locomotives had been coaled by means of tubs hand-loaded from the coaling stage with the sloping roof, nearest the camera in the left hand view. This was replaced early into Southern Railway days with the massive concrete hopper that lasted until the end of steam. The concrete stumps supporting the old structure were still visible in the lower view some 40 years afterwards.

Author's collection and Tony Deller

Chapter 4

A RETURN TO NINE ELMS

It had always been my intention to return to Nine Elms after a period at Feltham, and that resolve was still foremost in my mind. In 1961 I was still only nineteen years of age and if I stayed at Feltham, would have another four years firing in the top link, doing the same type of work before I would be able to take my driving examination in 1965. Whilst I could look forward to some mainline work in the summer months of 1962, it was not enough to make me have a change of heart. So I decided the time was right to return, also working on the basis that my 1957 seniority was such that I would be placed in '3B' link, just below the 'Tavy Gang'. Despite this being one of the lower running links at the depot, it was still a running link all the same. Thus, towards the end of 1961, I duly applied for an '8C' transfer back to Nine Elms. I knew I would dearly miss working with Albert Soundy but the desire to fulfil my ambition of firing on the mainline was the driving force. As such on 5th February 1962, I once again walked down Brooklands Road, SW8 and entered Nine Elms depot at 8.00 am for the second time in my career, albeit five years later. I was looking forward to future footplate work with 'great expectations'; who the Dickens said that once before?

Looking back, at that moment it still enabled me to work on some of the older Southern locomotives that would all disappear forever by the end of 1962. This was to be the last year of operation of for a number of locomotive icons, namely the 'Nelsons', 'Schools' and 'Arthurs'. Already many Adams, Drummond and Urie locomotives had been spirited away never to be seen again and further purges would continue as the end of steam slowly became a reality. Whatever, this was February 1962 and not the time to dwell on such things as I embarked upon the fulfilment of my considered 'raison d'etre'!

Back at Nine Elms I found that I had dropped down to '3B' Link, my regular mate being a 1947 man, Bill Plumb. I learned also that '3B' was involved with quite a degree of preparation and disposal work, still it had to be endured before I could finally reach my ultimate goal, the top link. So on that first day I was subtly brought down to earth when given charge of 'V' No 30921 'Shrewsbury' to dispose and then put up the shed. When you had no driver booked, it was generally accepted you would check the locomotive and move it as required in order to take water and coal and then down on to the disposal pit the other side of the coal-hopper.

The next day did not yield anything that much better in terms of my mainline aspirations as it was spent on 'E4' No 32473 working the coal road-shunter, definitely a touch of 'deja vu'.

Later in the week I worked on 'BB' No 34067 'Tangmere' and 'LN' No 30850 'Lord Nelson', both now preserved. The latter, 30850, had badly leaking stays. This, I recorded, had caused the locomotive to fail at Nine Elms on 15th February 1962, possibly the last time it was ever in steam on the Southern Region?

At last, four days later on 19th February, came my first mainline trip since my return, down to Salisbury. We signed on at 3.43 am for '22' duty, my driver being Frank Morris. Our allocated locomotive was 'V' No 30912 'Downside'. After relief at Salisbury the locomotive would work through to Yeovil Junction before turning and returning to London. Our return working from Salisbury was '525' duty, relieving an up Exeter train that departed at 9.33 am and ran fast to Andover Junction and then Waterloo. We had Salisbury-allocated 'MN' No 35009 'Shaw Savill', which, despite a 7 minutes late start, saw us arrive in Waterloo 3 minutes early. With a maximum speed of 92 mph recorded, this was just what I needed and I returned home to Chertsey somewhat tired, but extremely satisfied. There was a repeat performance with both locomotives two days later, although this time I noted that the exhaust injector was not working correctly on No 30912 thus wasting water.

The same could not be said of events on 23rd February 1962, when we had No 30912 on the same duty. This time the fire was extremely dirty before we departed from Nine Elms and after leaving Waterloo we struggled down to Woking with low water and steam pressure. Normally we had 35 minutes to wait in either the carriage sidings or on the Up Through, until the 5.40 am to Bournemouth passed. On this occasion I was firing to Bert Fordery and on arrival at Woking he requested we be put back into the East End sidings where there was a small engine requirement facility. Once over the small pit as much clinker and dirty fire was removed from the firebox and the ash-pan cleaned in the short amount of time available. With a reasonably fresh fire and a clean ash-pan we were soon back in business as we climbed away from Woking with the 6.36 am into St. John's cutting towards Brookwood. Again on the Up 'MN' No 35009 performed admirably, despite an 11 minutes late start.

Early in March I worked the 7.54 pm down to

Nine Elms locomotive, Class MN, 4-6-2, No 35014 'Nederland Line', pauses at Brockenhurst where driver Jim Robinson Senior and his fireman Peter Roberts are seen in this rather atmospheric photograph.   *(Photo Peter Roberts collection)*

Basingstoke with 'Standard 4' No 75078. The Up working was on 'LN' No 30857 *'Lord Howe'* with a train of 20 vans. What a pleasure to work one of these locomotives on the mainline at last.

Later in March, I had a 'local day' on 'M7' No 30039, a very nice little engine I recall. Even so I was with top link man Sydney Bracher, working empty stock between Clapham Junction and Waterloo. It was somewhat reminiscent of working with Tom Oxenham, for both men had the same worrying disposition. Sydney Bracher had the habit of constantly chewing his nails and then spitting them onto the footplate, I used to tell colleagues there were more fingernails than coal dust to sweep up when working with him. This was followed by successive day trips down to Woking on both 'V' No 30921 *'Shrewsbury'* and No 30936 *'Cranleigh'*, travelling over the East Putney line were indeed a pleasure. Around this time I recorded one of the few occasions I worked with the then 'Royal Train' driver, Bill Cornish. What a nice man he was, indeed, words cannot adequately describe such people that I met during these times.

As I mentioned earlier, in 1962 the 'Nelsons', 'Schools' and 'Arthurs' were coming to the end of their illustrious working lives and every opportunity to work upon them was, for me, something special. Indeed all three classes were held in high esteem by the majority of enginemen.

Towards the end of March I recorded another trip with Bert Shuck, this time on 'V' No 30902 *'Wellington'*. This was on a Basingstoke to Waterloo stopper, the return working of the engine from Yeovil. Sadly the regular 'Schools' locomotives that were used on this, No '22' duty, were beginning to be replaced with Standard Class '5' engines and the occasional 'West Country / Battle of Britain', although fortunately not entirely. A later account, see page 79, of working the 'Atlantic Coast Express' in the summer of 1962 was for me a most memorable experience.

At the beginning of April I was booked with Ernie Doust to work '491' duty, a fitted freight from Nine Elms Goods down to Salisbury. After signing on at 8.45 pm, we prepared the engine, 'BB' No 34068 *'Kenley'* and made our way light to Nine Elms Goods to pick up our train. I recall that it was rather foggy as we started away, sometime after 10.30 pm. Initially our progress was hindered by adverse signals and of course the fog, however as we made our way westwards, conditions marginally improved and we could at last get under way. The schedule showed us booked to run non-stop, however the delays had certainly caused us to use more water than normal, so, as was the practise, I checked the tender's capacity by using the water cock located on the driver's side of the tender. This was as we ran through Hook. Nothing showed! Now this was indeed bad news in terms of making Salisbury without stopping, so after duly reporting the fact to the driver I was somewhat surprised by his response. He blamed me for wasting water during our delays and then astounded me further by saying we would not be stopping at Basingstoke to fill up. Whilst I was still a young Fireman at the time, I had enough experience to know that we could be in serious trouble if delayed any more, for once past Andover, there was no opportunity to take water before Salisbury. Fortunately, there were no more delays and we made good progress. I made sure I kept the boiler water level high in the glass. Sure enough after passing through Porton the injector failed due to there being nothing left in the tender. I immediately told the driver, who having verified the water level in the boiler, appeared unconcerned. Now the immediate problem was that without the injectors working, I had no control over the steam pressure which naturally increased until the safety valves lifted. This in turn used up the existing water in the boiler at a far greater rate. Clearly it was the driver who was responsible for the situation that we were in, we just had to get to Salisbury and a water column. If that were not possible, I would have no option but to throw the fire out and save serious damage to the boiler. Fortunately, with the distant 'off' at Tunnel Junction, we ran directly into Salisbury's Platform 4. By now all that was showing was a quarter of glass with the engine still blowing off furiously. Salisbury men were waiting to relieve us, so after explaining the situation, we made our way to the mess room to await our return working, milk tanks, to Clapham Junction Kensington sidings via the East Putney line from Wimbledon. Very little was said between us as we sat down and consumed our tea and sandwiches. I realised that we had been lucky, for it could have ended up as a far more serious situation outside Salisbury. Our up working was without incident, 'MN' No 35015 'Rotterdam Lloyd' making relatively light work of the heavily loaded milk tanks.

Some weeks later I had the pleasure to work a week with old friend, Charlie Sutton, again out of Nine Elms Goods, 2.00 am to Basingstoke Yard. We had a variety of locomotives Monday, 'Q1' No 33014; Tuesday, 'S15' 30837; Wednesday, 'S15' 30503; Thursday, 'Q1' 33012 and Friday, 'S15' 30839. The return working was quite interesting with a Standard Class '5'. The train, the 6.37 am from Basingstoke to Waterloo, was an all stations stopper to Woking, then Weybridge, Walton, Surbiton and Waterloo. Probably one of the very last steam services that still served these local stations.

In mid-April, after just two months, I left Bill Plumb in '3B' and moved into the 'Tavy Gang', with a new driver, Walter (Wally) Finch. Wally had joined the Southern Railway in 1938. It was soon apparent that, unlike me, Wally was not interested in 'the job'. Despite this, we struck up a good working relationship and I recorded a number of good runs with him during the period I fired to him.

Thursday was traditionally known as 'Boat Train' train day, although of course this was not the only day such traffic would run to and from Southampton Docks. On one occasion I recall firing to Wally Finch when we worked down to the New Docks with Nine Elms allocated 'WC' No 34094 'Mortehoe'. I recorded the locomotive was in fine condition, and a period of bad coal at the depot she steamed freely and ran very well during the down trip. Depending upon the further requirements of the rolling stock, we would sometimes work back (ECS) to Clapham Yard, normally via the East Putney route or into Clapham Loop. However, on this occasion the stock was needed later in the day and instead we were instructed to take the engine, tender-first back 'light' to Eastleigh.

We left the docks via Millbrook and made our way to Eastleigh where we were brought to a stand at the semaphore Home signals. In those days there were four upper quadrant arms on the gantry. Up 'Main', 'Local', 'Romsey Loop', plus a 'Calling On' arm. After a few minutes, the 'Calling On' cleared, but Wally never responded. I indicated that we had the signal to proceed. Wally then informed me that this was not our signal, but applied to the 'Dorset Sidings' that ran adjacent to the Up line where we were standing. I reasoned that was not the case, simply because there was

no traffic in Stoneham sidings. Wally was still not convinced, so I offered to walk to the box and clarify the situation with the signalman. I was about to set off, when he enquired, "Where will that signal take us?" "On any of the three routes available, but they will be occupied", I replied. "All right we'll go" he responded, although clearly still uncertain. Sure enough, as we passed beneath the signal-box, we were turned into the Romsey Loop (then Platform 1) where there was a DEMU standing towards the end of the platform. Wally openly confessed to me that he had never seen that particular signal operated in the whole of his railway career.

Another memorable trip to Southampton Docks was when firing for the day to 1919 Engineman Len Nash. Our booked locomotive was a WR 'Standard 5' No 73029. It certainly looked in nice condition, resplendent in BR Brunswick green standing outside the shed, most unlike the black Nine Elms allocated series of the same class. As we began to prepare the locomotive I started to have early concerns that something was amiss. The fire bed was failing to respond to my normal method of preparation, this despite the cleanliness of the fire, ash-pan and brick arch. Once we had run light engine and arrived at Waterloo ready to head our Boat Train, I decided to voice my concerns to Len. He looked at the fire and whilst the steam pressure and water level were in order for the start of what was booked as a run he made little comment other than, "We'll have to wait and see"! Clapham Junction came and went and we were in dire straits as we began climbing up through Earlsfield towards Wimbledon. The boiler just failed to make steam and necessary use of the injectors immediately worsened the situation. Already the pressure had dropped back to 150lbs with the water down to a quarter of a glass as we approached Raynes Park. Needless to say our progress was extremely tardy!

Western Region 'Standards' could, for some reason, give vacuum brake problems if ever pressure dropped back this far. However the brake gauge still indicated 21" of vacuum despite only 145lbs pressure showing. Len examined the fire on several occasions as we continued towards Woking. With water precariously low we took advantage of the slight falling gradient at Weybridge. Eventually we passed through Woking around 40mph with the signalman anxiously looking out of the box.

Still we managed, just, to maintain 145lbs pressure climbing the bank beyond the station, although we had lost even more speed by the time we passed Pirbright Junction. Again there was some further respite that Len was able to advantage of as the gradient eased at milepost 31 and we dropped down through Deepcut towards the Basingstoke canal aqueduct, we gained a few extra precious pounds pressure and the bonus of a slight increase in water level. Surprisingly little was said on the footplate throughout the journey, for we both knew what we had to do to maintain any progress. Slowly then we made our way, juggling between using what steam there was to continue running and that needed for the injectors to keep the boiler water at a safe level. At Litchfield tunnel, it is then downhill all the way, we were travelling at 30-35 mph, although even when running on what was a favourable gradient, the locomotive still failed to respond, despite long periods with the regulator closed. We were so late when we finally arrived at the docks, it's a wonder the gates weren't locked shut and the ship had sailed without us. What a trip, certainly one of the hardest I ever encountered in my career. Later we ran light engine to Eastleigh depot where Len made out a 'Driver's Repair Card'. Naturally a report was also required due to the substantial loss of time. As the fireman, I heard nothing.

But then, some weeks later after signing on duty, I was walking up to the shed when I heard my name being called, it was Len. "Hello", he announced, "I've been looking for you'. Len went on to tell me that the engine we had that day was found to have a cracked blast-pipe and was immediately withdrawn from traffic at Eastleigh for repairs. Reason enough for all the problems that we encountered on the day for sure. His next words were a compliment indeed, for he told me that he personally could not have fired the locomotive any better than I had on the day. Praise indeed at the age of 20, which naturally also left me feeling on top of the world. As for Brunswick Green Standard '5's, I'll have a black one any day.

One Saturday in the height of summer, Wally and I worked one of the many extra trains required to Bournemouth West. The popularity of the south coast resorts in Kent, Sussex, Hampshire, Dorset, Devon and Cornwall and consequent extra trains, made great demands on the Southern Region London depots, these provided all the locomotives for the services. Equally all the rolling stock , like the locomotives, had to be used to its absolute maximum. The whole operation was a credit to the 'unsung hero's' in the diagrams office of the day. It was indeed somewhat like a precision military movement, almost every available pathway used during this period. Consequently this meant that various intermediate signal-boxes were brought into circuit. We could sometimes see in the distance, the smoke of the train in front as we made our way south.

On the day in question, we duly made our way to Bournemouth West with a 10-coach train, stopping at Brockenhurst, Sway, New Milton, Hinton Admiral, Christchurch and Pokesdown. The locomotive, a 'Standard 5' was in good condition and we were diagrammed to return with the same locomotive. As such I decided to keep the fire-box full, as the engine was steaming extremely freely on the down run and not to touch the fire during the short period we would have in the depot. With small coal I therefore damped the fire on arrival, reducing the steam pressure whilst we stood for a short period in the West station. Shortly afterwards

the stock was taken up to the carriage sidings and we were able to run light engine and turn on the Branksome triangle. Time enough to push forward a bit of coal in the tender and then make a quick can of tea. Then it was back to Bournemouth West ready for a hasty return to Waterloo, quite a tight diagram. The return working was clearly intended to get the stock repositioned for another 'Down' service the same day. As it turned out, this was the one and only occasion during my time as a fireman that I never stopped at either Bournemouth Central or Southampton Central on the same train, in fact New Milton was the only booked stop on the way up.

Just before departure I gave the fire a lift under the door with the dart that instantly brought it back to life. Then we were away, climbing the bank out of Bournemouth West through the same pine trees that had given the name to the never-to-be-forgotten 'Pines Express' of the old Somerset & Dorset line. With clear signals we ran through Bournemouth Central at restricted speed then on to New Milton. Perhaps surprisingly, only a very few people actually joined the train, despite the fact that we were running non-stop to London. Clearly there were more people starting their holidays than ending them at this time. Once away we again made good progress passing through Southampton Central on time and then, having climbed the bank with ease, we were signalled onto the 'Local' at Worting Junction and down through Basingstoke.

Travelling between Winchfield and Fleet, Wally told me that he was going to stop for water at Woking, due to the fact that the tender water gauge was not working. He was most concerned that we would not have enough to get us to Waterloo having, of course, not taken water at Southampton. Now, running fast, without delay and without excessive steam loss via the safety valves, means we were running quite efficiently in terms of both water and coal consumption. This was the situation but Wally was not convinced and stop we most certainly would.

However I had other ideas, so whilst Wally continued to lean out the cab window, I decided to have a look in the tender and check the water level. We were running at about 65 mph, nothing too drastic, so as we passed beneath one of the overhead semaphore gantries and with few bridges ahead until Farnborough I nimbly climbed up over the remaining coal onto the back of the tender and peered into the tank through the filler hole. As I thought, slightly less than half a tender, then in no more than 20-30 seconds I was back on the footplate. Naturally Wally was quite concerned with my 'acrobatics' and told me that he would not have allowed me to go if I had asked, but I already knew that. Whatever, we never did stop at Woking and continued on to Waterloo in good time, a quite remarkable trip. On arrival and to prove the point, I took the dart and climbed up onto the back of the tender, the official way this time and dipped the tender, revealing to Wally about a quarter of tender's capacity was still available.

Above - 'BB' No 34057 'Biggin Hill', one of six of the class named after the wartime aerodromes, seen at Southampton Central with the Brighton to Plymouth service, whilst in the background a 'LN' heads a New Docks to Waterloo 'Boat Train' in 1959.

Right - 'WC' No 34093 'Saunton' passing Semley with the down 'Atlantic Coast Express', 12th August 1964.

Top left *- Old friend Robin Bell, on a 'Class 3' 2-6-2T, at Waterloo in January 1965.*   *M. Dominey*
Top right *- Bert Hooker looks every bit an Engineman on the footplate of Class 'D' No 1737.*

G. Lawrence collection

Below *- Engineman Harry Tester and I are seen on the footplate of Drummond '700' No 30694 at Feltham Yard in 1960.*

B. Tipping

Above - *Engineman 'Dickie' Thomas alongside 'MN' 35030 'Elder Dempster Lines' at Nine Elms depot in 1962. Always smartly turned out, for me he epitomised the end of an era of loco-men who maintained an immense pride in their work, their skill and appearance, right to the end of their long illustrious footplate careers.*

W. Smith

Top right - *A number of years before my practical driving examination in 1965, Dick Thomas with Fireman Ellery seen at Waterloo on the footplate of 'WC' 34018 'Axminster'.*

W. Smith

Centre right - *1918 gentleman Driver Charlie Sutton at Salisbury with the 9.00 am Waterloo to Exeter in charge of Exmouth Junction based 'WC' 34030 'Watersmeet' in 1959.*

Bottom right - *David (Duncan) Davis back on the footplate again when steam returned. Always knowledgeable about locomotives and Nine Elms days, he often spoke about recording details of those times.*

Departure from Waterloo destination Handborough.

Passing Feltham West End. Certainly a different scene exists today from the same vantage point.

Fireman J Lester

BRITISH RAIL.

ASSISTANT GENERAL MANAGER SOUTHERN REGION WATERLOO	ASSISTANT GENERAL MANAGER WESTERN REGION PADDINGTON

JOINT SPECIAL NOTICE NO. 41 AGM

26th January, 1965.

SATURDAY, 30th JANUARY 1965.

FUNERAL OF THE LATE SIR WINSTON CHURCHILL.

In connection with the funeral of the late Sir Winston Churchill a private special train will run from Waterloo to Handborough and return from Handborough to Paddington.

FORWARD JOURNEY - WATERLOO TO HANDBOROUGH.

Empty train to form the Private Special :-

	Arr.	Dep.
Stewarts Lane		11 00
Stewarts Lane Junction		11 05
Clapham Junction (No.49 Siding)	11 14	11 47
		T.L.
West London Junction		11 49½
Vauxhall		11 54
Waterloo (Up Main Through Inner	11 57	12 01
Home Signal) No. WB 101		
Waterloo (Platform No. 11)	12 03	

This empty train is authorised to work with an engine at each end between Clapham Junction and Waterloo Up Main through inner home signal (WB.101), where the leading engine will be detached and the rear engine will then propel the empty train to Platform No. 11. The Yard Foreman, Waterloo, will take charge of the propelling movement.

Formation leaving Stewarts Lane Junction :-

Engine
Pullman Brake Car No. 208 (Brake leading))
Bogie Van 2464   )
Pullman Car "Carina" (kitchen trailing)   )
Pullman Car "Lydia" (kitchen trailing)   ) Gangways connected.
Pullman Car "Perseus" (large Saloon leading))
Pullman Brake Car "Isle of Thanet" (brake   )
                                   trailing))

The empty train will be placed in Platform No. 11 with the rearmost (i.e. buffers stop end) door of van 2464 opposite a point indicated by a distinctive white mark on the platform.

Engine No. 34051 to work the 13 28 Private Special train from Waterloo :-

	Arr.	Dep.
Nine Elms Shed		12 45
Loco Junction	12 50	12 55
Vauxhall		R.L.
Waterloo (Platform 11)	13 00	

SHEET NO. 1 (Contd.)

PRIVATE SPECIAL TRAIN.

		Engine to carry special Headcode throughout as shown below
Waterloo (Platform No. 11)	13 28 Down Windsor Local Line	
Barnes		
Twickenham	13 39	
Staines Central	13 46	
Virginia Water	13 56	
Ascot	14 04	
Wokingham	14 14	
Reading Spur Box	14 24	
	14 33	
Reading Main Line East (W.R.)		
Down Branch Home Signal No. 187	14 34	14 36
Reading General	M.L.	
Didcot East Junction	14 39	
Didcot North	14 59	
Oxford	15 00½	
Yarnton	T15 12L	
Handborough (Up Platform)	15 17 15 23	

Take up W.R. Driver Conductor P. Talbot and W.R. Conductor Guard H.F. Simmons.

Train to be signalled as a Class 1 train.

After the cortege has left the station the train to remain in the Up Platform until departure at 16 20.

S.R. engine will return "light" leaving Handborough at 15 50 for Oxford, turn and take water, thence to Nine Elms via Reading Spur. Oxford dep. 17 00.
Reading Spur arr. 17 47C

Formation leaving Waterloo :-

Engine No. 34051 ("Battle of Britain" Class)
Pullman Brake Car No. 208 (brake leading))
Bogie Van 2464   )
Pullman Car "Carina" (kitchen trailing)   )
Pullman Car "Lydia" (kitchen trailing)   ) Gangways connected.
Pullman Car "Perseus" (large Saloon leading))
Pullman Brake Car "Isle of Thanet" (brake trailing))

Stopping Point.

At Handborough the private special train must be brought to a stand with the centre of the engine footplate opposite a point indicated by distinctive white posts with white lights situated each side of the Up Main Line to indicate the place at which the train must stop.

The distance from the centre of the engine footplate to the centre of the leading door of Bogie Van No. 2464 through which the bearer party with the coffin will alight is as follows -

99 feet 5 inches.

Standby Engines.

Standby engines to be provided as follows :-
Staines Central - No. 34064 "Battle of Britain" Class - Chimney towards Reading - S.R. to provide.
Reading General - W.R. Diesel Locomotive D.1028 - W.R. to provide.

JOINT SPECIAL NOTICE NO. 41 AGM (Contd.)

Train Reporting.

The time at which the train has left, passed or arrived, must be reported from the following stations and signal boxes as follows :-

Waterloo	)	Reading East Main	)
Staines Central	) To be reported immediately to	Didcot East Jc.	) To be reported immediately to
Wokingham	) the T.S.O. Woking	Oxford South	) Divisional Control
Reading Spur	) for transmission	Handborough	) for transmission
	) to H.Q. Control.		) to H.Q. Control

Driver and Guard of the Private Special Train.

Driver A. W. Hurley   - Waterloo to Handborough
                             (Conductor) Reading Spur to Handborough

Fireman J. C. Lester   - Waterloo to Handborough

Guard W. H. Horwill   - Waterloo to Handborough
                             (Conductor) Reading Spur to Handborough

Inspectors

S.R. Divisional Inspector A. G. Pay and W.R. Chief Inspector W. J. Richards will travel with the train throughout. Inspector Pay must enter in his report the number of persons (other than Railway Officers) who travel in the private party.

S.R. Motive Power Inspector W. F. Meal will travel on the engine footplate throughout.

RETURN JOURNEY - HANDBOROUGH TO PADDINGTON.

W.R. Diesel Locomotive D.1015 to work return journey Handborough to Paddington to leave Oxford 14 30, Handborough arrive 14 42 and be stabled in Up Siding. To be attached to train at 15 55.

	Arr.	Dep.
Handborough (Up Platform)		16 20
Yarnton		
Oxford	16 26	
Didcot North	T16 31L	
Didcot East Junction	16 42	
Reading General	K16 43½L	
Twyford	T16 58L	
Maidenhead	17 02	
Slough	17 07	
Southall	17 12	
Westbourne Park	17 30	
Paddington (No. 8 Platform)	17 35	

From Up Platform. The train to carry Number 1Z00 and be signalled accordingly.

Formation leaving Handborough :-

Diesel Locomotive D.1015
Pullman Brake Car "Isle of Thanet" (Brake leading))
Pullman Car "Perseus" (Large Saloon trailing)   )
Pullman Car "Lydia" (Kitchen leading)   )
Pullman Car "Carina" (Kitchen trailing)   ) Gangways connected
Bogie Van 2464   )
Pullman Brake Car No. 208 (Brake trailing)   )

JOINT SPECIAL NOTICE NO. 41 AGM (Contd.)

Driver and Guard of the train.

Driver	J. H. L. Brown
2nd Man	L. G. Altringham
Guard	H. F. Simmons

Inspector

Chief Inspector W. J. Richards will travel with the Private special and must enter in his report the number of persons (other than railway officers) who travel.

H.Q. Chief Running Inspector W. A. Andress will travel in cab of locomotive.

Standby Engine.

Reading General - W.R. Diesel Locomotive No. D.1028.

Train Reporting.

The time at which the train has left, passed or arrived must be reported from the following stations and signal boxes as shown below :-

Handborough	)
Oxford South	)
Didcot East Junction	) To be reported immediately to
Reading East Main	) Divisional Control for transmission
Slough, Paddington	) to H.Q. Control.
Southall West Junction	)
Paddington	)

Empty train after working 16 20 Handborough to Paddington :-

	Arr.	Dep.
Paddington		17 50 DCL
Subway Junction		M17 58L
Portobello Junction		CL
West London Yard		18 04
North Pole Junction		18 08
Kensington (Olympia)	18 15	18 30
Latchmere Junction		18 37
Longhedge Junction		18 40
Stewarts Lane Junction	18 43	18 45
Stewarts Lane	18 48	

W.R. Diesel Locomotive to Kensington.
S.R. Engine from Kensington.

S. D. WARD	H. M. LATTINER
ASSISTANT GENERAL MANAGER SOUTHERN REGION	ASSISTANT GENERAL MANAGER WESTERN REGION

SHEET NO. 4 (FINAL.)

BRITISH RAIL
SOUTHERN REGION

TO:- (SEE ATTACHED)
    Fireman J.C. Lester,
    C/o. Shed Master,
    <u>NINE ELMS</u>.

My ref : TS.

LINE MANAGER,
SOUTH WESTERN DIVISION,
19, WORPLE ROAD,
WIMBLEDON, S.W.19.

8th February, 1965.

FUNERAL OF THE LATE SIR WINSTON CHURCHILL.

I am glad to show you copies of letters exchanged with the General Manager.

Copy of letter dated 5th February, 1965, from General Manager, to
<u>Line Manager, South Western Division.</u>

"I have received a letter from the Duke of Norfolk which reads :-

" This is just a line to say thank you for all your help during the past days.

I know many people joined together, and through you, please thank any of your people I may have missed out, as naturally, I have not met all who were concerned in a memorable week.   I am most grateful.

Yours sincerely,

Norfolk. "

So many were concerned that I cannot attempt to mention all by name, but may I join with the Duke in thanking you for all the splendid work which went into making this memorable occasion a success."

. . . .

Copy of letter dated 8th February, 1965, from Line Manager, South
<u>Western Division, to General Manager.</u>

"I have read with pleasure your letter of the 5th February.

On the South Western Line we have all felt privileged to have been so closely associated with this memorable occasion and thereby to have had the opportunity of each making in our own way our personal tribute.

Your message will be gladly passed on."

. . . .

Not only is this praise deserved by all who had a part in planning and running the special train but all along the line of route can feel they played their part.

Added to their responsibilities were the large numbers of well-wishers who thronged stations and vantage points all along the route.   This feature of the journey made a deep impression.

Well done all !

There were hundreds and hundreds of the footplate crews historically associated with working on steam hauled trains from both Waterloo and Nine Elms Goods Yard to numerous destinations in the South West of England from 1838 to 1967. Below the wonderful arch at Waterloo station is the stain glass coat of arms of the 'London & South Western Railway' and surrounded by the names of the counties that the company served. The lines in many of these counties were part of the extensive route miles over which Nine Elms Enginemen had an intimate working knowledge over many years.

Unusually 'Engineman' was a term almost specifically used by the Southern Railway formed in 1923 and a special brass cap badge was produced during this period, somewhat similar in many ways to the rather handsome copper badge of the old 'London Brighton & South Coast Railway'.

Many of the older more senior drivers at the depot still wore these badges, no doubt issued to them in early Southern Railway days, as such these badges became quite a coveted possession for many and as the years went by they became extremely difficult to obtain.

I became the proud owner of one at the tender age of seventeen and wore it with immense pride. Sadly I lost it one day whilst working on Class 'M7', No. 30245, when running past Nine Elms depot with empty coaching stock to Clapham Yard. It was actually consumed by the locomotive's fire when drawn into the firebox: having been accidentally knocked off my head in the cab. In the aftermath of this incident I remember how I felt at the time, devastated! Incidentally the same locomotive is now preserved in York Railway Museum.

The use of the term 'Engineman' within our fraternity, certainly when speaking of senior men, was a genuine token of the high esteem in which they were held by their subordinate colleagues. There were indeed some fine men, 'masters of their craft' and as a fireman in the late fifties and early sixties it was an education and a privilege, to work with such men.

It was equally interesting during these times to observe that there was a continued rivalry dating back decades between many of them. I can certainly remember the banter between Alf Hurley and George Holloway when I was firing in the 'Top Link'.

The photograph above is of my 'second' 'Engineman S.R.' cap badge, kindly given to me by an old friend, it restored my pride once more and I am eternally grateful to have to this day.

The Nine Elms Enginemen's Reunion

Jointly Tim Crowley and I organise the annual 'Nine Elms Enginemen's Reunion'. The first one started in 1999 and is now a continued successful gathering of many associated active and retired Enginemen!

Seen is our dedicated 'Nine Elms Enginemen' headboard that we have been proud to place on the smoke-box front of various classes of locomotive in memory of all these men. Perhaps one day in the future we will see it on the front of a main line steam hauled operation over 'Southern' lines as a tribute to many of the fine 'Enginemen', known and unknown.

We now have a dedicated Nine Elms website that is linked to our reunions and has become extremely popular since it opened. Log in on www.nineelms.svsfilm.com and take a trip down to the Elms, it's still there really! Look forward to seeing you!

Right The 'Nine Elms Enginemen' headboard, fittingly seen here on 'WC' No 21C123 'Blackmoor Vale'.

John Fry

Above - *My 1960 photograph of Adams radial 30582, standing at Chertsey, a special event, particularly for myself on the day. Before joining British Railways, my local station's history and the fact that it also had a locomotive depot dating back to the late 1840s, had fascinated me from an early age. Amongst the earliest locomotives that worked the line were, Beattie '0298' 2-4-0WT, Adams Class '0415' 4-4-2T, and 0-4-4T 'T1' and 'O2' and later of course Drummond 'M7', tank engines.*

Left - *Jim Lester in front of No. 65, an old 'South Eastern Railway' engine dating back to 1899, on the Bluebell Railway.*

Steve West

Chapter 5

'PILOT GANG'

Six months later, in October 1962, I was promoted again, this time into the 'Pilot Gang' with a new regular driver, William 'Bill' Turner. Bill had started in April 1934 and was a staunch trade-unionist, upholding the long-term traditions of the 1880 founded Associated Society of Locomotive Engineers & Firemen (ASLE&F). I learned a lot with Bill, for he was amongst the finest of men I have ever known. His high standards became your high standards in every way and the year ahead proved to be both an absolute pleasure and an education.

The driver's extensive route knowledge in the Pilot Gang, meant that a diverse amount of 'spot' running work would be allocated accordingly. As such the gang had a fair degree of spare work to encompass anything extra that the depot would naturally cover.

One day in December 1962, I found myself booked on 'spare' without Bill, who had been booked to cover a vacant position on the day. This was always a likely occurrence as I will describe the numerous drivers that I worked with whilst in the 'Pilot Gang'.

On the day in question, the Running Foreman came into the cabin and asked me if I actually had a driver booked with me? When I replied I did not, he said, "Can you look after 30585 and put her up the shed". I queried the number immediately, my own knowledge of loco numbers being quite good and I honestly thought he had made a mistake. He smiled and indicated that it was the correct number. To my utter amazement, there standing outside sandwiched between two pacifics, was this little '0298' 2-4-0WT. As I took charge of her a number of loco-men came to have a look, no doubt the very first time that they had ever seen such a locomotive before.

I subsequently discovered that two of the last three remaining Beattie, 1874 built, 'well tanks' had in fact made, what can only be described as an 'epic journey' under their own steam, from their almost lifetime depot, Wadebridge (72F) in Cornwall, to Nine Elms. It was with immense pleasure that after taking water I moved the loco down under the coal hopper. The coal-man asked where he was going to put the coal, such was the diminutive size of the bunker. "Just put a little bit on the cab roof", I said. Once on the pit road, I climbed up on top, broke up the coal and shovelled it into the narrow bunker space. I decided not to clean the fire until the engine was turned and we were later in position over a pit in the shed. It was far better that the small firebox wasn't cleaned until movement of the loco was complete. What an event, what a privilege to work on such an historic locomotive, certainly a highlight of my footplate career.

Shortly after this winter set in with a vengeance. For weeks on end at the end of 1962 and into 1963 there was massive disruption on the railway system. In what can only be described as arctic conditions, lines were blocked, and engines and trains became buried in snowdrifts. Passengers had to be

When I took this photograph of '0298' No 30585 in 1959 at Wadebridge (72F) depot, little did I ever think that I would actually work on the same locomotive in Nine Elms depot some three years later.

rescued from remote rural lines that had become impassable and trains were being cancelled in large numbers.

As the New Year continued, conditions did not get any better. Temperatures plummeted and remained close to or below freezing for much of that January. This put paid to any hope of a thaw and then as more snow storms swept the country during the course of the month, the disruption of the railway system continued unabated. It is a remarkable statistic that much of England remained continuously covered by snow from Boxing Day 1962 until the first week of March 1963.

This then is the background to a trip I made in January 1963 when booked to work a 'Boat Train' back up from Southampton (Old Docks) to Waterloo. Bill Turner and I had worked a train down during the early hours of the morning, with a Standard '5' and were booked to work back up to London. On the way down, it had been snowing heavily, the conditions being really bad, but somehow they had managed to keep the tracks open in the old docks, and we were able to make our way across Canute Road despite the atrocious conditions.

Unfortunately, after we'd arrived and taken water, we were left standing for quite some time in the bitter cold. There was deep snow everywhere, so much so that it was even difficult to get off the locomotive. Then, when attempting to top up the boiler water level, I found both the injectors would not work as they had become frozen. There was enough water in the boiler at the time, but we knew that if we were unable to get them working again, we would not be going anywhere at all.

Bill and I searched around the footplate and found some dirty old hand-clothes that we then soaked in paraffin and oil. We then wrapped them around the injector bodies and set fire to them. A bit drastic, but it did the trick, as in a short time water started to trickle through the injector overflow pipes restoring them to working order, thereafter I regularly used them intermittently to avoid any further problems. Eventually the shunter arrived through the snow and we then moved slowly along the dock lines and finally dropped back on to our train that was inside one of the dockside sheds alongside the ocean liner. We had 10 or 11 coaches including two Pullmans, and although officially a 'Boat Train', we were given a special stop order to call at Eastleigh, Winchester, and Basingstoke to pick up anyone who wanted to travel. Obviously this was due to the fact that there were so few trains running on the main line due to the conditions. Once clear of the docks we made reasonable progress calling at Eastleigh en route. We had just restarted the train after the Winchester City stop and were continuing the climb on up towards Micheldever with the engine having to work really hard in the frightful conditions. After passing Winchester Junction and coming around the curve into the cutting before Wallers Ash Tunnel, we were confronted by a wall of snow. The whole of the cutting was simply full of drift snow such that we could not see the tracks, it really was the most incredible sight. There were two choices, stop and not go on any further, or go for it and hope that we would be able to punch our way through whatever was there. Bill decided on the latter, we would attempt to get through.

He opened the regulator fully, turned on the sanders, and literally launched the train into this mass of snow. Within seconds, the engine was totally enveloped, you couldn't see the sky, you couldn't see out of the cab windows, there was snow everywhere. The engine started to labour, even with Bill increasing the cut-off, we gradually got slower and slower until I was beginning to think that we were going to come to a halt. Then we burst out of the bank of snow into reasonably open track again. What the experience was like in the train I can't imagine.

After that, conditions eased a little and whilst remaining extremely cold, we eventually made it to Waterloo without further incident. Despite the fact that we had started with a tender full of coal, it was now completely empty with just enough fire in the box to get back to Nine Elms. When writing this years later, I still think those were the worst conditions that I ever experienced in the whole of my railway career. I had worked something like 18 hours and at the end was absolutely exhausted. Bill, who was a solid union man, told me to take the next day off in order to recover, which I gratefully did.

During my time in the Pilot Gang, I had the opportunity to work with many different drivers other than my regular 'mate' and indeed on many different locomotives. I have attempted to record some of the more interesting times and events. My records show that as time went by, I was working on certain locomotives more often than others that were allocated to the depot. This was certainly the case with '70A's original Bulleid 'WC' No 34094 'Mortehoe' as I recorded another trip on this engine on the 11th May 1963 with Charlie Sutton. This time after preparing the locomotive for 'Spl. 2' duty, we ran light engine, unusually tender first, from Nine Elms to Clapham Junction. Then, after changing the lamp and disk boards, we went round to Kensington Olympia, via Latchmere Junction, where we picked up an Old Oak Common conductor. In fact we never did have a train, as we were booked to run light engine all the way to Banbury, travelling via High Wycombe and Princess Risborough. This was part of the joint GWR/GCR route of years gone by. On arrival we were relieved and the locomotive continued on towards Birmingham, eventually working a 'Warwickshire Rail Club' special later that weekend.

Yet another fine Nine Elms Engineman was 'top link' Driver, Richard (Dickie) Thomas. Although I knew him quite well, I only fired to him on one occasion, 5th March 1963 on number 2/31 duty, signing on at 3.45 am. Fortunately it was down the mainline with the 5.40 am to Bournemouth on 'BB' No 34071 '601 Squadron'. We had a mixture of thirteen vans and coaches. We returned with the 10.30 am up on 'MN' No 35010 'Blue Star'. Although there was forty odd years between our ages I relished all the railway conversations that I had with him. It was equally a pleasure to work with men like him who still raised the levels of footplate work by their total professionalism, something I cherished then and still do today.

On another occasion in May 1963 I was booked along with another 'top link' man, Fred Streeter. We were on the 3.00 pm Waterloo to Exeter as usual being relieved at Salisbury. On the day the allocated locomotive was 'MN' No 35016 'Elders Fyffes' an engine I recall in good condition. After preparation, it was customary to always to clean the boiler front and footplate in general before coming off shed and running light engine to Waterloo. As such the engine looked splendid when we eventually arrived at the top of our train of eleven coaches, an easy load for a 'Merchant Navy'. Once under way, our first station call was Basingstoke with the engine responding immediately to the fire I had prepared earlier. Indeed, such was the ease of firing, linked to the way it was being driven, that I decided to improve the cleanliness of the back-head, so between the still necessary occasional spells of firing and observing the road ahead, I rubbed the copper and brass fittings with brick dust I kept in an old tobacco tin in my bag. After our brief stop Basingstoke it was Andover Junction next, by which time footplate looked superb. However, in all this time Fred never said a word and I certainly felt my endeavours weren't really appreciated.

With the final leg of the journey to Salisbury almost complete I wiped everything down for the last time, before running in with the fire in good condition, full up, just the way the Exmouth Junction firemen liked it.

On arrival the relieving Exmouth Junction driver climbed onto the footplate, looked around and said "'As 'er just come off a Royal"? "No," said Fred casually "my mate always gives them a clean up like this on the way down"! After we had taken water and the coal at the back of the tender shovelled forward for the onward journey, we collected our coats, bags and the tea-can of course. Walking down platform 5 Fred put his hand on my shoulder and said "Well done mate, that was wonderful". At that time it really was a great feeling to confidently work the footplate of such trains, the occasional praise also making it all the more worthwhile. For the return we relieved on 34018 at platform 2, taking the 6.38 pm to Waterloo, this time with a modest nine coaches load. Despite having a very dirty brick-arch I recorded it as a free steaming locomotive.

Of those that can remember events back at the start of 1965 many will recall the standby duty performed by 1947 built 'BB' No 34064 'Fighter Command' as the support locomotive used during the initial stages of the Winston Churchill funeral arrangements. During my time at Nine Elms, 34064 had been a Battersea based 'Battle of Britain' for many years - I will be talking much more about the funeral train and the privileged part I had in its working a little later.

'Top Link Engineman' Fred Streeter seen here with his Fireman, Ron Petrie, on 'WC' No 34010 'Sidmouth' at Salisbury on his last day at work after 52 years service. Born in 1898, Fred had started on the LB&SCR at Battersea Roundhouse in 1911. He later transferred to Nine Elms, retiring on 27th June 1963.

R. Petrie collection

Earlier, 1946 class mate 34051 'Winston Churchill' had been a Salisbury based locomotive most of its working life, although it did however carry a 'temporary' 70A shed plate when performing the duty of hauling the funeral train from Waterloo to Handborough in Oxfordshire. Incidentally, in response to various magazine articles in which it is suggested that 34051 was in fact several other engines in disguise, let me put the record straight. Utter nonsense. From my personal involvement with the preparation I know this not to have been the case, confirmation being that for the week leading up to the special working, 30th January 1965, driver Alf (Lew) Hurley and I were removed from all duties in order to perform any work required on the locomotive in connection with the fitting staff. There certainly was no evidence of any 'makeover' whatsoever and rest assured I would have seen it from where I was standing!

But to return to the stand-by engine, 34064. What set this particular machine apart from its contemporaries was that it had emerged from Eastleigh Works in 1962 fitted with a Giesl oblong ejector in place of the normal multiple-jet blast-pipe exhaust system. This also allowed a spark arresters to be fitted without causing any undue impediment on the steaming qualities of the locomotive, as previously had been the case.

At the time, this modification was a surprise to almost all interested enginemen, bearing in mind steam traction was definitely in decline, plus the fact that the modification program of the original Bulleid locomotives was still being pursued.

As such all the enginemen at Nine Elms were given a handout entitled 'Locomotive No 34064. Notes on Giesel Oblong Ejector fitted with Spark Arrester', dated 9th May 1962 that explained the principles of the ejector and basically how it worked.

On the 26th January 1963, another 'top link' man I was booked with was Harry Patchett. Personally I did not consider him to be in the same league as that of his contemporaries, but I have included the trip as a point of interest in terms of the locomotive's performance on the day. Signing on at Vauxhall at 5.20pm, for '525' duty, we made our way to Waterloo to work the 6.00pm Salisbury and found 34064 'Fighter Command' on the front, this was instead of what would normally have been a booked Merchant Navy diagram. At this time Nine Elms had received an amount of ovals for fuel, basically cemented coal dust, causing numerous

Seen here outside the 'Old' shed at Nine Elms. 34064 'Fighter Command' is being prepared as the standby engine for the Sir Winston Churchill's funeral train in January 1965. The head-code is for the route Waterloo to Reading. The locomotive later ran light to Staines where it stood in the down loop.

Tony Deller

JC/iT

9th' May, 1962.

Locomotive No. 34064. Notes on Giesl Oblong Ejector,
fitted with Spark Arrester.
_____

The numerous experiments carried out in the past on unmodified
"West Country" and "Battle of Britain" class locomotives to prevent spark
emission have failed because the addition of a spark arrester has always
ruined the engines' free steaming qualities. The reason for these failures
has been that the multiple jet exhaust arrangement could not be made to
produce enough draught to overcome the extra resistance to gas flow
through the boiler caused by the spark arrester plates or mesh.
Sharpening the blast did not solve the problem and led to a reduction in
the locomotive's power output. A more efficient exhaust device obviously
had to be sought.

Recently a new, highly developed design of blast pipe and chimney
of Austrian origin has become available know as the Giesl(rhyming with
diesel) Oblong Ejector. Its application to No. 34064 is expected to
finally overcome this difficult and important spark arresting problem.

The Giesl Ejector's greater efficiency compared with the multiple jet
exhaust arrangement (itself an excellent one in many respects) makes it
fully capable of overcoming the resistance caused by the mesh of the spark
arrester. It is adjusted so that it does this without spoiling the
steaming, which remains at least as free as before. The locomotive is
less prone to make black smoke and now does its job with a slight reduction
in the blast pipe pressure (or back pressure on the pistons).

Seven nozzles, with blower jets placed between them, are arranged
in line to exhaust into a narrow chimney round which a hinged fine wire
mesh spark arrester is fitted. A valuable feature of the design is
that the chimney is fixed in perfect alignment with the blast pipe, thus
eliminating one frequent cause of bad steaming. The chimney is also made
in three sections and can be simply removed for access to the superheater
tubes and can then be just as simply replaced with its alignment guaranteed
to be correct. The main and blower nozzles need cleaning at each 'X Day'
examination.

In the Giesl design the exhaust leaves the chimney top with much
greater velocity, so that this, combined with the narrow frontal area of
the chimney and its extended height, is likely to make a far greater
improvement to the smoke lifting of these engines than any of the earlier
alterations made with this object specifically in mind. This special
advantage is quite incidental to the main purpose of the experiment which
is to avoid spark throwing.

Theoretically the ideal locomotive chimney is tall in relation to its
choke and early locomotive engineers realised this and proportioned their
chimneys accordingly. This ideal was departed from as boilers grew larger
and larger until it was lost sight of altogether and good accepted practice
became far from theoretically correct. The Giesl Oblong Ejector may be
considered as being seven correctly shaped chimneys "rolled into one" so
that ideal proportions are retained and adequate capacity is ensured. In
any exhaust arrangement there is bound to be some waste of energy and the
principal losses occur during the mixing of exhaust steam and gases and
at the chimney top as kinetic energy or energy of motion. The total losses
are much lower with the Giesl compared with the multiple jet chimney but
whereas the mixing losses are lower with the Giesl and much higher with the
multiple jet, the reverse is true of the chimney top loss and it is this
fact that makes the exhaust pass clear of the locomotive with the Giesl
chimney though it often tends to hug round the locomotive with the
existing arrangement.

The Giesl Oblong Ejector may be considered as the ultimate solution
to the exhaust problem on steam locomotives, combining, as it does, the
best of the theory and practice on a subject upon which a great deal of
effort has been concentrated in the past.

Alf Hurley tops up the big-end of 'WC' 34048 'Crediton' in Bournemouth Central loco, in readiness for the return working to Waterloo.

steaming problems. The effect of the quality of the coal dust, plus the cement combined to reduced the heat created. Not so on 34064, once under way the exhaust was having a different to normal effect on the fire as the engine got into its stride. On this particular trip I found the fire burned quite ferociously to say the least, although it resulted in the need for almost continuous rounds of firing, just to keep the fire in good shape. The bonus was that the engine steamed prolifically in the circumstances. Overall the engine was generally in good condition and after our scheduled stop at Andover Junction and continuing west towards Salisbury, I was amazed at the speed through Grateley, over 60mph. (Grateley was also near the summit of a long 1 in 165 climb). Incidentally, the return from Salisbury was with number '6' duty, on one of my old regulars, 'MN' 35016, '*Elders Fyffes*'.

Continuing with another tale from the winter months of early 1963, on 9th February 1963 Bill and I booked on at Vauxhall at 7.23 am for 82 duty, going first 'pass' to Surbiton where we relieved the crew on 31612 in the yard. The first thing that we noticed was that the bottom wash-out plug on the Fireman's side was blowing very badly. Now this situation could be very serious, as the condition of the plug is an unknown quantity in terms of the cause of the blow. Following the last wash-out, it was possible the plug had been incorrectly put in place, cross-threaded maybe, or perhaps just in finger tight and never properly tightened afterwards. Theses plugs had quite a fine thread and were also tapered to ensure a good seal. No washers were used with this particular arrangement.

The fact that the previous crew had been prepared to work all night long with the locomotive in this condition is hard to believe, but clearly that is what had happened. Bill certainly didn't like the situation at all and immediately looked in the engine's tool-box to see if there was a spanner to fit the square top of the plug. One was found, after which he cleaned the area around where the plug was blowing and then applied some vacuum oil to the exterior thread. "If you want to get off while I do this, you can", Bill announced. I decided to remain where I was and watched whilst he applied some pressure on the spanner. As the plug moved, so the blow subsided until it stopped completely. Of course, should it have blown out at any stage after coming off the shed that morning, the consequences for the footplate crew were hardly worth considering. Whatever, all was now well and we took a small freight train round to Hampton Court, shunted the yard, then after returning to Surbiton, worked a pick-up freight to Feltham via Chertsey.

On the 14th March 1963, came yet again another trip on 'MN' 35016 '*Elders Fyffes*', this time with 1915 'top link man Fred Damer. We went down to Salisbury with the 9.00 am with a relatively light load of 10 coaches, totalling just 314 tons. The engine was still in fine fettle and we had a trouble-free run. After a somewhat lengthy meal break of two hours, we worked the 12.58 pm back to Waterloo on 34051 '*Winston Churchill*', that I recorded as being in very poor condition, in particular with uneven valve events. Despite this, I noted that it was steaming freely. What a difference there was two years later with the engine when used on the funeral train in 1965.

Here is a story from the past again concerening 'MN' No 35016 that was told to me by my old friend and colleague the late Charles (Charlie) Holter. At Nine Elms, during Southern Railway days, Charlie's regular engine was in fact 21C16 '*Elders Fyffes*' then in original condition. The incident occurred whilst working an up fast from Bournemouth to Waterloo as they were passing through Woking. Apparently when re-applying the injector, unbeknown to him the valve that controlled the pep pipe, used to wash down the footplate, had vibrated open and the pipe being under extreme pressure literally flew about the cab. As such Charlie received scalding hot water full in the face. Fortunately Charlie's driver quickly managed to control the situation and shut the valve, whilst his next action certainly saved the day. In those days, many of the drivers brought tea to work in bottles, namely of the old 'Johnny Walker' whisky type, square in shape, so they would lay flat in the tray above the fire-hole door. Thus they could drink their tea either during a meal break or when running. The driver immediately emptied the contents of the luke-warm tea all over Charlie's face in order to relieve the pain. Charlie insisted that they continue to Waterloo, whereupon on arrival he was taken straight to St Thomas's hospital. The Doctor later told Charlie that in the circumstances his driver's action had certainly saved him from more serious injury.

On most occasions I really enjoyed the variety of the drivers with whom I was booked to work. However, I recall a rather fractious event, when booked along with Charlie Partridge (whose nickname at the depot was 'The Bird'). He was a starchy character who had very little to say on the first day when we signed on at 2.55 pm for 30/32 duty. We prepared our own locomotive for the turn, 'MN' No 35024 '*East Asiatic Company*', then ran light to Waterloo and worked the 4.35 pm, down 'The Royal Wessex' to Bournemouth Central. As ever I cleaned the boiler front and washed the footplate before we departed. As we made our way west, I continued to keep the dust down by occasionally watering the footplate after sweeping up. Sometime after Woking and approaching Brookwood, he called me over and told me sit in his seat. He then proceeded to spray the whole of the footplate with the 'pep' pipe particularly under the seat where I was sitting. "How do you like that?" he said in quite a nasty tone. I failed to understand what he meant in the circumstances, but he continued, "I don't like water sprayed under my legs like that so don't do it anymore", this in an equally aggressive manner!

Now I hadn't done anything like that, nor would I ever, but it was enough for me. So during the rest of the journey I failed to sweep the floor under him or damp the coal dust on his side of the cab. By the time we arrived at Bournemouth his side of the footplate was a mess whilst my side was fine.

The relieving Weymouth crew must have wondered just what was going on as they took charge of the locomotive. "Oh dear 'ave you two fallen out?", asked the Driver. With my coat, bag and tea-can I was off the engine and was making my way down the platform with Charlie Partridge in hot pursuit and calling me to come back. Needless to say I ignored him and continued on to the small mess-room where he eventually caught up. I told him in no uncertain terms

that I would not be treated or talked to in such a way and that his manner both extremely rude and unnecessary. I reminded him that all he had to do was ask in a reasonable fashion to limit the water used in damping the dust and there would not have been a problem. I was so incensed I continued that if he wanted another fireman he'd better phone the depot and get one!

To be fair he did apologise, the heat of the moment was over. We returned to Waterloo with the 'last Weymouth' on 34037 '*Clovelly*', without, I might add, any repeat performance of the down journey. I now understood him and he understood me. Actually I was booked to work with him for the next two days, both of which were quite pleasant and civil and I like to think that we parted on reasonable terms.

At Nine Elms for a period in 1963, the coal hopper was out of commission, locomotives being turned and then mechanically coaled from the emergency 'stack' located in the triangle situated in front of the old Nine Elms Works. This huge heap of coal had seriously deteriorated during the lengthy time it had been stored on the ground, being subject to the vagaries of the weather. My friend Alan Wilton used to refer to it as the 'Nine Elms - Super Sifted - Never Glow Coal', although his succinct adjective never even did it justice, in reality it was far worse than that. Everyone experienced difficulty attempting to time trains due to this coal and consequent lack of steam. During a weeks work down with the 5.30 pm Bournemouth, like other colleagues I suffered some difficult times on the footplate. I honestly believed that this was the beginning of the end of steam in 1963 and in the circumstances, linked to certain home problems at the time, I decided to leave the railway service totally disillusioned, a letter to this effect was duly submitted to Mr. Gilchrist, the Nine Elms Shed-master.

To describe that week, here is an example from the first of those days. Our locomotive on the 5.30 pm was 'BB' 34077 '*602 Squadron*'. Despite my best attempts at firing, we arrived at Basingstoke very much the worse for wear. Tuesday was much the same again, although clearly there was steaming a problem with this locomotive, as even with poor coal we should have done better. On Wednesday it was much the same, however when passing through Farnborough and still struggling with the abysmal poor quality coal, a huge lorry tyre, obviously picked up off of the 'stack' came down completely blocking the shovelling plate and any further access to more coal. After quite a protracted period of endeavour with both the coal-pick, shovel and rocker-bar, plus Bill's able assistance, the tyre was eventually dislodged but not before the existing fire had but all burnt away leaving me with the almost impossible task of trying to restore the fire bed with coal you could have grown potatoes in! On arrival at

Waiting for the 'Right-Away' at Bournemouth Central George Bowen gives a hint of a smile from 'WC' No 34008 'Padstow'.

Basingstoke, Bill calmly instructed me to wash down the tyre and locate it behind the driving position on the tender plate. During what little time we had left I attempted to restore the depleted pressure, fire and water before we set off again. We were relieved at Eastleigh and took the tyre with us, standing it in the corner of the mess room whilst we had a can of tea and a sandwich. We eventually returned to Nine Elms with the tyre still accompanying us on the footplate. Bill was somewhat quiet throughout this episode and I did not seek an explanation of his intent.

The next evening, Thursday, walking up the platform to relieve the preparing crew, I could not believe what I saw. A different engine for a start, stacked with 'real' coal on the tender. Standing alongside the cab was Mr. Downes, the Motive Power Superintendent. He duly acknowledged Bill and climbed on to the footplate. Turning to me he said "Well fireman, what do you think of this? I've heard all about the great difficulties that you've had recently from your Driver, including the incident with the tyre, which Bill sent to my office in Worple Road, Wimbledon". Then with a smile he produced my resignation letter from his pocket and said, "Do you think you might reconsider your resignation?" Pointing to the fire-hole door he said, "Can I put it in the filing cabinet?" I immediately agreed and as it went up in flames we shook hands before he left us. Life was back on track again as we made our way down to Basingstoke that evening, this time with steam to spare, I might add. Bill later explained everything that had happened, plus the subsequent intervention of Mr. Downes that had improved things immensely during what was an extremely difficult time at Nine Elms.

Another great Nine Elms character was Harry

Tester. Due to his rather lean appearance, the nickname 'Bones' was sometimes given to him by some of the young firemen. It wasn't said in a derogatory manner at all, as Harry was an extremely popular engineman. He also had a slight stammer as I recall and would have us in fits of laughter in the cabin when telling a story with his dry, nay parched, sense of humour.

Sometime in 1959 as a 'Passed Cleaner', I had finished my duty for the day around 8.30 am, having signed on the previous night just after midnight and I decided to ride up to Waterloo on the 9.30 am Bournemouth engine on my way home. The Driver was Harry, along with his then regular mate Peter Kilford, whose father was also Nine Elms top link driver. When we arrived at Waterloo Harry asked me if was going to ride down with them to Woking, knowing that I lived at Chertsey. Although quite tired I agreed, whereupon Harry insisted that I take the shovel and show his mate how to do it. "He's ber-ber-ber-bleedin' useless", he said in his inimitable fashion. Well it was another chance to gain a bit more mainline experience at the age of seventeen, so I took the opportunity and had a nice trip arriving in Woking in fine fettle. Harry then tried to persuade me to continue but I was desperately in need of sleep so declined.

When I was eventually booked to fire to him on the mainline, we had just coupled to our train at Waterloo and were making ready on the footplate for the trip to Bournemouth semi-fast when the guard approached the cab to provide the details of the load. Harry was full of his usual banter, then turning to the guard in all seriousness, he remarked, "Do you know that history is being made today"? "No" replied the guard, by now equally quite serious. "Well" said Harry, "We've got Driver Tester, Fireman Lester and Guard Chester in charge of the train"! Never a dull moment with Harry and his wit, what a wonderful chap.

Now Harry Pope was very different character altogether for he had a somewhat dubious reputation. Hardly deemed one of the elite of Nine Elms men, he was renown for excessive speed and equally a purloiner of other footplate crews' tea.

Now we had some speed merchants at the Elms, but there is going fast in a controlled and professional way and then there was Harry's way! His regular firemen certainly had their work cut out on the shovel when Harry was performing on the regulator. Now double-heading was quite a rare event on trains from Waterloo, however I remember one day when Harry was required to take a Standard class locomotive down to Basingstoke depot and for whatever the reason, Control decided that it was to go down coupled to the front of a Basingstoke stopping service. The actual driver of the train was none other than Charlie Letchford, a real fast runner indeed, the thought of the two of them at the head of a train was unimaginable. Word soon spread and as the time for departure of the Basingstoke service from Waterloo approached a number of men assembled near the triangle, located by the old Nine Elms Works, to witness the passing of the train.

First the sound was heard as both locomotives accelerated from Vauxhall, then they came into sight going like a blur with just five coaches hanging on behind, what a sight indeed, they must have been two minutes early at Clapham Junction at the rate they were going!

Harry's extremely bad habit of drinking footplate tea without invitation led a number of crews to seek some sort of revenge on him. Let me explain, when preparing your locomotive, the last thing to be done prior to leaving the shed was to make a can of tea. Several cups of tea were something that you certainly needed, having just spent the best part of an hour making up the fire of a Bulleid pacific, plus various other associated preparation tasks and indeed there was the journey ahead to consider. As such it was recognised that a can for making the tea was an essential part of a footplate crew's equipment. Harry's reputation went before him and if he was to travel on the footplate, as many did when travelling to Waterloo from the depot, either the full tea can would be hidden out of sight or if it had already been almost consumed, then the remains would topped up with water from the boiler. Now in those days boiler water contained 'TIA', a brown coloured water softener, added to the tenders of the locomotives in briquette form. No doubt this was most unpleasant to drink as well as likely to have some dire effects. Whatever, Harry would still drink it with relish, seemingly oblivious of the real contents and to the delight I might add of those looking on!

One of Harry's regular mates, Lenny Holloway, complained bitterly that Harry would greedily drink more than his fair share of the tea and decided to do something about it. When we saw what he had done everyone was highly amused, for he had had a hasp riveted to his tea can and lid with a small padlock attached, thus denying Harry access when Lenny's attention was occupied elsewhere!

Harry Pope and Mike Roberts are here seen on the footplate of 'MN', No 35012, 'United States Line'.
Mike Roberts collection

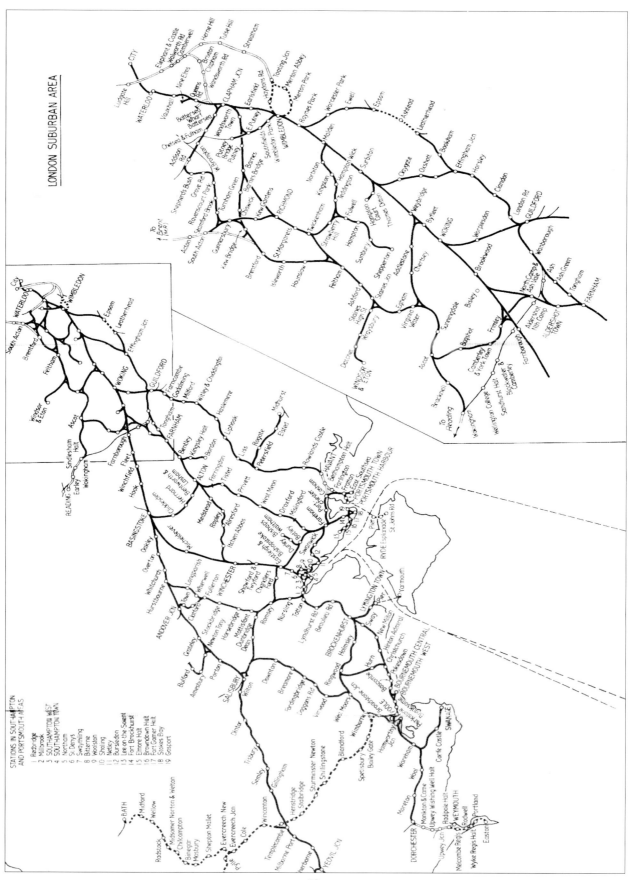

LONDON SUBURBAN AREA

STATIONS IN SOUTHAMPTON
AND PORTSMOUTH AREAS
1 Redbridge
2 Millbrook
3 SOUTHAMPTON WEST
4 SOUTHAMPTON TERM.
5 Northam
6 St Denys
7 Swaything
8 Bitterne
9 Woolston
10 Sholing
11 Netley
12 Bursledon
13 Lee on the Swent
14 Fort Brockhurst
15 Elmore Holt
16 Browndown Holt
17 Fort Gomer Holt
18 Stokes Bay
19 Gosport

Chapter 6

'TOP - LINK'

As the summer of 1963 gave way to autumn, I was aware that more senior firemen were being rapidly promoted, due to the policy of passing men for driving duties as soon as possible. I had just turned 21 years and already I was a senior fireman in the 'Pilot Gang'. It was hard to believe that a year had passed so quickly whilst firing to Bill Turner. We had had some difficult working times together, particularly during the winter months. The period of poor quality coal had also made life both demanding and frustrating. Having said that, we had overcome those times by working closely together and looking back now, I considered we were a good combination. I recall also the quiet times sat on the footplate, when we would discuss all aspects of the locomotive and the rules and regulations concerning signals and protection. I am indebted to Bill to this day for his guidance.

Such were the good times being booked with Bill, it caused me to have certain reservations about my impending promotion into the Top Link. In the circumstances I checked who the likely drivers with whom I would eventually work, none I felt of the same stature as Bill. I had determined the next likely promotion date would be in December, so it was a big surprise in October when I was told that I would be promoted to the top link on the 21st of that month. I had obviously made a mistake in my appraised move date

and immediately went to discover who my next driver would be. A couple of colleagues were in the lobby at the time, one said that I had 'Good fortune', or words to that effect, in typical unrepeatable Battersea linguistic terms! Who was Alf (Lew) Hurley, I really didn't know? I had certainly never fired to him during my time at Nine Elms. Whatever, prior to my impending promotion, everyone I met agreed that he was indeed a fine senior engineman, dating back to 'South Western' days in 1917. As it turned out his regular fireman had suddenly resigned, thus throwing my promotional calculations out the window.

Our first day's work together was rather uneventful, however little did I know at the time it was actually the beginning of a memorable two and half year period on the footplate with yet another 'special' engineman. That first day, we signed on at 5.46 am for '23' duty and prepared our locomotive, unusually 'MN' No 35024 'East Asiatic Company', as this was only to work the 7.20 am stopper to Basingstoke. Apparently the booked 'Standard Class 5', No 73082 'Camelot' had failed on shed.

During the same week we worked the 5.40 am to Bournemouth Central every other day, returning with the 10.30 am to Waterloo. The first of these trips was on 'WC' No 34010 'Sidmouth', that I recorded as not steaming too freely. Later examination revealed the

Bournemouth West departure, Alf cautiously starts 'WC' No 34048 'Crediton' up the bank towards Branksome and the junction. Note the plate on the cab roof warning that the smell of 'Aniseed' would indicate a hot inside big-end. Others indicated the aroma of 'Garlic'.

This photograph of Alf and myself, was taken at Bournemouth West in the winter of 1963. The locomotive was 'BB' No 34079 '141 Squadron', for many years a Ramsgate (74B) allocated engine. Many of the first 'modified' engines were immediately transferred onto the Eastern section of the Southern, releasing the later built BB's to work on the South Western.

engine to have been fitted with a spark arrester, generally the source of the problem on a number of occasions. The return working was a trouble free run with 'MN' No 35019 'French Line CGT'. Uniquely this was the only one of the class to have a script written nameplate.

The original Bulleid locomotives were indeed rather special and would run extremely freely, more so than their rebuilt counterparts. I recall working the 5.00 pm Salisbury - Exeter service with 'BB' 34070 'Manston' one evening. Fresh out of Eastleigh works, it was one of the finest Bulleids that I ever worked on. We arrived at our first stop Basingstoke, somewhat before our scheduled time, such was the absolute ease that it had run. We were both impressed, what a superb locomotive!

I had had some good times since returning to Nine Elms, with my early months in the top link

extremely satisfying. Our working relationship and friendship made life on the footplate a pleasure. Alf was a very fit man, even at the age of sixty-one he would regularly take the shovel and hand over the locomotive to my charge. A much appreciated gesture of trust and confidence.

Despite my 'elevated' status in the top link, we would still occasionally prepare our own locomotive, which was not such a bad thing, inasmuch you could set the fire and have the engine exactly how you wanted it ready for a main line trip, sometimes based upon previous experience of that particular locomotive that I had recorded. The bulk of the dirty disposal work was, fortunately, left to others, I'm pleased to say!

Another of our allocated 'Merchant Navy's' I worked on in those first couple of weeks, this time down to Salisbury at 3.00 pm, was 'MN' No 35017 'Belgian Marine'. This locomotive was equally quite unique, not because of anything to do with the name, but because the firebox was not fitted with thermic siphons. It was rather strange to see this huge brick-arch spanning the total width of the firebox, whereas, with a normal firebox, there were actually three individual brick arches linked across the firebox. Whilst the prowess of the class for free steaming was generally attributed to the siphon action and the increased boiler water circulation, there did not appear to be any deficiency in the locomotive's steaming capacity whatsoever.

On the 1st November, Alf and I were again booked to work the 3.00 pm Salisbury – Exeter, this time the locomotive was a 1960 rebuild, No 34090, '*Sir Eustace Missenden - Southern Railway*'. When the original Bulleid engine was named at Waterloo in 1949, after the General Manager of the Southern Railway during the war, it was indeed a special occasion, a tribute in fact to all those employees who managed to keep the Southern Railway running despite persistent enemy aircraft attacks. That day in November 1960, was the first of two occasions that I worked on the locomotive when it was suffering reported steaming problems. On both occasions I examined the smoke-box during preparation and found the spark arrester mesh clogged up with a carbon deposit that then inhibited the blast effect on the fire. In this condition it also allowed carbon to build up on the multiple jet blast pipe that then affected the exhaust steam interaction with petticoat pipe. All sounds a bit technical really, but by ensuring both the mesh and the blast pipe head were kept free of carbon the steaming qualities of the locomotive improved significantly. As such I would regularly check the interior of the smoke-box during preparation, however with engines that were already prepared, this was not possible. Our trip down to Salisbury was not too bright and I recorded the engine maintaining steam at just 200lbs, as such I was unable to improve on this below par performance.

Some time later we were booked to work the Sunday 8.10 am Jersey Boat Train to Weymouth, being relieved at Bournemouth Centra, with same locomotive, 34090. During preparation I noted the carbon deposit was quite substantial so I duly removed and cleaned the front arrester grill, then the side grills and finally the multiple blast-pipe top. After running light engine to Waterloo, we were met by Inspector Plummer, an old friend of Alf's, who indicated that he was riding down with us due to reports of bad steaming and subsequent loss of time with an up Exeter service. On this occasion the engine performed extremely well and the 48 miles running non-stop to Basingstoke was as good as any rebuilt 'Battle of Britain'. Inspector Plummer expressed his surprise at the engine's steaming capabilities, whereupon I enlightened him as to what I had done in the smoke-box during preparation time. He thanked me

for the information and recorded the details in his little 'Black Book'. Obviously he had seen enough and left us on arrival at Basingstoke. Some time later Alf told me that he was quite impressed with the intervention, and in fact had submitted a report detailing the action that I had taken.

During a time when Alf was on annual leave, I had another 'top-link' driver, Dick Turpin of 1918 vintage. Dick's role in the link being as the holiday-relief man. We were booked with the 10.30 am down to Bournemouth and whilst coupled to our train at Waterloo and waiting for departure time, Inspector George Bolland came to the cab and spoke to him. He produced some paper work and then climbed aboard along with another gentleman, who was introduced as Mr. Helmuth.

I learned during our brief conversation that he owned several large garages, a sign advertising his local garage could be seen on the wall of the south sidings outside of Waterloo. He was a very well spoken man, the quality of his clothes and shoes reflected his good education and position. I offered him my seat for the journey but he politely refused. The trip down to Southampton was quite straightforward with the engine performing extremely well. Very little was said throughout the trip, however as we were approaching Southampton Central, where he was getting off, he came over and thanked me for an enlightening footplate experience. He indicated that for many years he had wanted to make such a trip and pointedly added that he wouldn't mind a driver's job, but likened my work shovelling coal "as similar to feeding buns to an elephant...endless"! Just before he alighted, he had some words with Dick, before both he and Inspector Bolland climbed down and made their way along the platform. The water column was immediately swung round to top up the tender during the station time available and in no time at all we were away on the second leg of the journey. As the engine got into its stride once again Dick called me over. "Mr Helmuth gave me £5", he said, "we'll share it between us when we get to Bournemouth". That was a generous amount and I duly received my £2.10s after we had arrived. Later in the week I was approached by George Bolland who got straight to the point. "Did Mr Helmuth give your driver anything at Southampton the other day", he enquired? Innocently I replied, "I don't really know, you'd have to ask him". Clearly George was looking for his own share, despite the fact that we had done all the work. Now 70A's Dick Turpin was certainly no modern day highwayman, however I couldn't see him prepared to "stand and deliver" anything in the circumstances. Unbeknown to me at that time, a year or so later I would be sitting in front of George Bolland on my driving examination!!!

Chapter 7

'BLACK-SHEEP' PACIFICS

Having worked down to Bournemouth one day, we were relieved at the Central station and after meal-break were booked to relieve an up Weymouth train. The majority of these London-bound trains normally had a portion attached to the rear, thus strengthening the onward load to sometimes twelve and thirteen coaches. The actual rear portion had previously arrived from Bournemouth West and was then pulled back into a siding alongside the locomotive depot, usually by the station pilot tank engine, in readiness to be attached to the rear of the in-coming Weymouth. It was quite a unique piece of shunting, all the passengers remaining seated whilst it was executed, with great precision I might add.

On the day in question we were waiting for the front portion to arrive whereupon, not unlike Salisbury, water would be taken with the Bournemouth or Weymouth fireman responsible for the pipe. My responsibility would be to take the opportunity of shovelling as much coal forward as possible in the short time available.

The eventual arrival of the train revealed at the head, 'WC' 34043 'Combe Martin', one of 71B's (Bournemouth) best - or not, as was the truth. Now it was common knowledge to us, that three of the 'West Country / Battle of Britain' locomotives were not particularly good steamers, 34011 'Tavistock' and 34065 'Hurricane', both Nine Elms engines at that time and guess the other one, 34043 'Combe Martin'.

Les Pitchell, who regularly fired to Len Rickard in the mid 1950s, recently told me that 34053 'Sir Keith Park' was another with similar problems. Despite their combined expertise and endeavours, he recalled they had the same experience on any number of occasions they had worked on that locomotive. Interestingly, 34053 was a relatively early rebuild in 1958, whether or not it overcame the steaming deficiency I don't really know, as my records do not reveal any footplate trips on the locomotive.

Back at Bournemouth Central and having arrived with just six coaches, the Weymouth driver indicated to Alf in his lovely Dorset drawl "Ers not a lot a good s'know", so we knew what to expect. The fact that another six coaches were being attached onto the rear as we spoke, just made things 'better' in terms of the challenge ahead. Soon whistles were blowing and we were away, first stop Southampton and then non-stop to Waterloo.

Leaving Bournemouth Central, through the single bore but lengthy Winton Road over-bridge, the route climbs, levelling out towards the old Boscombe station before dropping sharply through Pokesdown and on into Christchurch. In such as short space of time, I always found that it possible to take stock of the condition of the locomotive, particularly when running non-stop to Southampton. Indeed by the time you had crossed the River Avon girder bridge, where the old original branch line from Ringwood joined the new main line, and were seriously into the bank up towards Hinton Admiral you had a pretty good idea of things to come.

On occasions with certain locomotives it was necessary to adopt a different firing application, particular those renowned as bad steamers. Whilst Bulleid boilers, with their thermic siphons and large grate area, did not normally give any problems, there were times when something extra was required and today was clearly was one of those times. The good old, 'light, bright and tight' firing method needed to be employed, most unusual on a Bulleid for sure. Once over the top of the bank and having passed through New Milton and Sway, the locomotive was only eased once the speed had increased, so the approach to Lymington Junction was in truth the first respite in terms of heavy working and what had been virtually continuous firing activity. Down through Brockenhurst at speed then climbing up towards 'Wood Fiddlely' crossing box, in the heart of the New Forest. Up through Beaulieu Road station then dropping sharply down through Lyndhurst Road, across Ashurst crossing then braking for the approach to Totton. During this time the locomotive had performed reasonably well, but still not quite right despite all the extra endeavours. Over the bridge that crosses the River Test that flows into Southampton Water and the large dock area beyond, past the little loco shed on the water's edge at Redbridge we continued to climb until passing Millbrook, before running into Southampton Central. Here more water was taken to top up the 5000 gallon tender and the remaining coal pushed forward against the tender's internal coal-door. Once away from Southampton, past Northam Junction and St Denys, the bank really started. Somewhat overloaded with twelve coaches behind a 7P / 5F rated locomotive, requires far more extension in terms of the way the locomotive is worked, certainly in comparison with a class 'Merchant Navy' 8P rating. Regulator position and cut-off determine the progress that will be made, add to that boiler pressure and the

Bournemouth's 'West Country' No 34043 'Combe Martin' at Shillingstone on the Somerset & Dorset line in 1959. 71B allocated 34040 – 34044 were all fitted with brackets on their tenders that enabled the S&D's tablet changer mechanism, specifically designed for operating over the route, to be attached.

scene is set. With a maximum pressure of 250lbs, there is a greater degree of leeway in terms of pressure that can be lost without undue affect on the performance, so far as the steam being applied to the steam-chest. On that day leaving Southampton, the fire, boiler pressure and water were right on the mark ready for the sustained heavy continuous working on the climb from Eastleigh to Litchfield Tunnel. Once into the bank there is no respite for over 20 miles, until Worting Junction is passed and where the line now drops down past Winklebury intermediate signals and on to Basingstoke. On this occasion the poor behaviour of No 34043 meant there was a need to turn off the injector to maintain boiler pressure, resulting in a gradual loss of water level. As we passed over the summit, pressure had dropped back to below 180lbs whilst the water was down to about half of a glass. This was quite exceptional in my firing experiences, bearing in mind the style of firing that I employed on the day. I can honestly say that I have never had a fire so continuously 'hot' whilst climbing the bank. My hands and arms were burning during each short round of firing, the engine's boiler should have been stuck at 250lbs such was the heat of the fire. As soon as the regulator was eased the pressure increased immediately, so much so both injectors were used to hold her back. On the falling gradient after passing Worting Junction, the engine ran absolutely perfectly, sitting on the red line all the way into London. I discussed this trip with Bert Hooker some time later, as I couldn't understand what was really amiss. He explained that some locomotives could not produce the steam required based on the way that they were being worked, irrespective of the firing methods employed. Once the demand for steam was slightly reduced, then the boiler would respond accordingly. Where the majority of the same class could cope, there were those few that could not, due principally to their general condition, this despite the endeavours of the crews.

An interesting observation surrounding these three original Bulleid locomotives, Nos 34011, 34043 and 34065, is that none were re-built. Equally all three were early withdrawals from traffic in 1963/64 compared with others in the class. They were also some of the lower mileage members of the class. Did their reputation have any bearing on the outcome of their eventual early demise or was it sheer coincidence?

In front of a gleaming 34051, Alf and myself pose for an unknown photographer. It had taken a week to prepare this and standby sister engine, 34064 to this state of perfection. On the train the engine performed as well she looked.

Mark Abbott

Chapter 8

THE SIR WINSTON CHURCHILL FUNERAL TRAIN

At the age of 22, I had been in the 'Top Link' at Nine Elms for about a year when my driver Alf Hurley and I, were called to the office of the Shed Master, Mr Gilcrist. There we were told we had been selected to work the forthcoming state funeral train. We were then briefed on the train running arrangements which had been carefully prepared to carry the coffin of the late Sir Winston Churchill plus his immediate family to Oxfordshire. Both Alf and I had earlier noticed we had previously seemed to be attracting an unusual number of visits from a footplate inspector on a variety of trains that we worked. Undoubtedly this was all part of the crew selection process.

Although we had been selected by the Southern Region management, two other top link drivers were designated as standby. These were George Holloway and Jerry Sartin, both fine Southern enginemen. Alf and I were informed that we were to be relieved of all duties for the week prior to the funeral, Saturday 30th January 1965, the time to be spent assisting with the preparation of 34051, the predetermined choice of locomotive. As such we spent the early part of the week with the fitters, whilst it was arranged that later in the week all three drivers were to be booked a 'route appraisal' day, one could hardly describe it as 'route learning' in the short time available. This was from Waterloo via Ascot to Reading and thence to Kingham, on the old Oxford, Worcester and Wolverhampton line.

Knowing the route was as critical a factor for a fireman as a driver in many ways, for it allowed good engine management, water conservation, economy and efficiency. I prided myself on my personal route knowledge, as I studied the lines over which I worked. In fact I was already intimate with the line to Reading South, including the Spur line, following earlier years working at Feltham depot in 1960 / 61 / 62.

In the circumstances I duly requested from the Shed-Master, that I too be permitted to accompany the trio and venture into foreign territory. This might now sound straightforward and under the circumstances sensible, but in reality it had never happened before, a fireman route learning. Somewhat liken to Oliver Twist asking for more! However the shed-master was no Mister Beadle and he fully understood and appreciated my request. The Chief Clerk was thus suitably informed and my name was placed on the 'Daily Alteration Sheet' accordingly. Even at this late stage in the story of steam traction, history was still being made.

I should add that the three drivers that I had the privilege of working with and would now accompany had all started with the LSWR back in 1917. Collectively they had almost 150 years of service, I can hardly imagine what my meage seven years meant. Whatever, I loved my railway work and did it to the best

Looking quite splendid, 'BB' No 34051 is seen coming off the merge near the corner of the 'New' shed built in 1910.

T. Deller

Left - *Frank Berry, an old friend and colleague of Alf Hurley. Similar in age they both went back along way. Frank progressed from the footplate and became on of the Running Foremen responsible for the locomotives at the depot. Towards the end of his railway career he took responsibility for cleaning and shed maintenance.*

Bottom - *Mr Gilcrist, shedmaster at Nine Elms at the time of the funeral train.*

Both: T. Deller

of my ability, always ready to take advice and learn from men like these. Now, after my own near 50 years service, I too can look back on some wonderful times.

But I digress, for the original trio, now a quartet, together travelled down to Reading South and then crossed the road to enter the somewhat grander Reading General station. We took our seats behind the WR driver on what was a normal DMU working. Before departure we spoke to the driver and explained the purpose of our journey. He assisted by leaving the connecting door open and explaining various features of the line en-route.

On arrival at Handborough, we were somewhat surprised at the poor condition of the station, extremely run down with flaking paint and rusted railings and fittings. How could anyone possibly deal with the required work to smarten up this rather sad little station in just a few days?

Water consumption was always going to be a vital factor on the day, not only throughout the journey but during the stand off time before departure and after arrival. The actual route miles to Handborough was comparable to a Waterloo to Salisbury service, a trip that was near the limit for the tender's water capacity so leaving little to spare. This was a major concern on the day. The plan to conserve water had to work well as we would be unable to refill the tender until we eventually backed into Oxford depot on the return.

The locomotive 34051 'Winston Churchill' had before this, been stored in semi retirement, fittingly within its home depot at Salisbury (old 72B), perhaps just waiting for this momentous occasion. At the appropriate time, actually the 25th January, it was moved up to Nine Elms and where for almost week a hive of activity ensued. No 34064 'Fighter Command' was similarly meticulously prepared. This would be the reserve locomotive, should anything untoward occur.

On the day of the funeral, the preparation of the locomotive, which had been beautifully cleaned during the past week, was deliberately left to Alf and myself. As was the custom, the headcode of the train to be worked from Waterloo was placed on the tender brackets, however, on this occasion three of the four special disc boards normally used on Royal Trains were

used, rather than the standard versions.

Normally the fire of a Bulleid pacific would be substantially built-up for a mainline service, thus providing not only the basis of a large fire to start either a Salisbury-Exeter or Bournemouth-Weymouth bound train, but equally it also helped conserve the essential tender coal capacity for those lengthy journeys. However this was no normal day, and great care was required in every aspect of preparation, particularly with the fire. Boiler control would be absolutely critical, steam, water, fire, smoke, all had to be correctly managed. Not too much, not too little, both Alf and I knew that timing was the order of the day.

When we left Nine Elms on that grey January afternoon, we had a boiler full of water and 150lbs pressure. The fire was deliberately small, but adequate, placed mainly under the door. On arrival at the country end of Platform 11 at Waterloo we stopped. It was not yet time to back onto the train, the vehicles for which were already marshalled next to the buffer stops. Whilst we waited, the three special disc boards were removed from the tender and duly positioned in the famous Churchillian 'V' for Victory formation on the front of the locomotive.

The diagrammed wait at the top of platform seemed eternal, 'a watched kettle never boils' they say. It certainly seemed that way to me. At the prescribed time, we then backed down onto the train and after coupling up and with steam heat on at 40 lbs pressure, it was time to perform. Blower cracked, ease the fire fully over the grate, steam pressure increasing slowly, 180, 190 to around 200lbs.

In the quiet, almost surreal surroundings of the normal vibrant station, I vividly recall the arrival of the funeral cortege. It was a very special moment, the sound of the shuffling feet of the coffin bearing guardsmen and then the closing van doors, station duties completed on time, 1.28 pm, no whistles or fuss, just a green flag silently waved by the Royal Train guard, Mr. W. H. Horwill.

Alf's light touch on the locomotive's whistle announced our imminent departure, as he then eased the 'Battle of Britain' class locomotive No. 34051 *'Winston Churchill'* and its train, consisting of five Pullman cars, *'No. 208'*, *'Carina'*, *'Lydia'*, *'Perseus'*, and *'Isle of Thanet'* and a Southern bogie PMV S2464, probably the last with corridor connections containing the coffin, away from the capital's largest terminus Waterloo,

Alf and myself Recorded by the official BR photographer on 26th January 1965.

Left - *Leaving Nine Elms depot and climbing towards the Engine Siding located alongside the down Local line.*

A Rowe

Above - *Plenty of exhaust steam is in evidence as 34051 progresses on to the down Windsor line en-route to Handborough.*

Above - *A steamy start across Westminster Bridge Road, sees 'BB' 34051 easing out of Waterloo's Platform 11.*
Bottom - *'BB' No 34051 is seen here approaching Vauxhall on the down Windsor local. Signs of an early round of firing is evident from the chimney.*

Approaching Richmond with 34051 now nicely responding to the occasion, it was a pleasure to be on the footplate. The locomotive could not have performed better throughout the journey.

bound for a small village station, Handborough, in Oxfordshire.

Needless to say with a 'cold' start from Waterloo, the fire required immediate attention and by Vauxhall I was already busy deftly delivering coal through the Ajax door. Pressure had remained static at 200lbs, but once passed Clapham Junction the locomotive was warming-up and the boiler started to respond to the regular small rounds of firing, 'light, bright and tight', text book stuff on the day. This train certainly wasn't the 'The Royal Wessex' or the 'Atlantic Coast Express'.

After crossing the Thames at Richmond and whilst on the approach to the platform at St. Margarets, I could see the semaphore distant signal for Twickenham was at 'Caution', despite the fact that we had a pre-arranged priority pathway. Not surprisingly this caused some concern on the footplate for Chief Loco Inspector, Bill Neal who was accompanying us. As speed was reduced, we were all looking ahead for the position of the 'Home', 'Starter' and 'Advance Starter' signals (section signal), the latter incidentally had the 'Distant' signal for Kneller located beneath it. All were in the 'Off' position, however I still recall the concerned looks on the signalmen's faces at the two Twickenham signal boxes, not knowing whether to give us a wave or not. It later turned out the distant, which was motorised I believe, had become defective.

Whitton Junction was passed, followed by Feltham Junction, where the familiar massive marshalling yard with its two humps came into view. On the far left lay Feltham depot the former bastion of Mr. Urie's locomotives and where during my time there his class 'S15' 4-6-0, 'H16' 4-6-2T and 'G16' 4-8-0T reigned supreme, now all sadly withdrawn after many fine years of service. As we approached Staines Central, the other splendid pacific, 'BB' No 34064 'Fighter Command' came into view, standing like a sentinel in the down loop. A friendly wave between both the footplates was exchanged, normally it would have warranted a customary blast on the whistle, but not today.

At the junction at the end of the platform we branched left, leaving the original 1849 line to Windsor & Eton Riverside on our right. Negotiating the tight 20 mph reverse curves we crossed the Thames again, then effortlessly gathering speed we passed over the crossings at Thorpe Lane and Pooley Green before travelling down through Egham, then we started climbing the bank, over Rusham crossing and up through Virginia Water past the triangular junction to Chertsey. Just beyond Knowle East, one of two intermediate signal boxes, I saw my mother and father on the railway embankment, witnessing, like many others, the passing of this once in a lifetime event. It was indeed moving to see such huge amounts of people lining the entire route, particularly many old uniformed soldiers, standing crisply to attention, saluting.

At Sunningdale, with its huge angular level crossing gates, we crossed the main A30 road and finally reached the top of the bank at the Gasworks sidings before proceeding down through Ascot, with its manicured ballast, clipped hedges and its six whitewashed platform edges, today hosting masses of people. Climbing again, we now passed the additional up line Race Platform, up through the avenue of rhododendron bushes toward Ascot West, where the winter quarters for Bertram Mills Circus were located. It was among the same rhododendrons one morning, that the 6.10 am Feltham Yard to Reading freight, hit a milk float on an unmanned level crossing. There were some dry cornflakes in Ascot that day !

The locomotive was performing beautifully, steaming to perfection with the 'monitor injectors' cut fine and the steam generator humming away contently. This provided the comfortable driving cab with electric

Left - *Chief Inspector Bill Neale.*

Bottom - *In the background Knowle East signals can be seen as we climb towards Sunningdale and Ascot.*
J. H. Bird

lighting located in all the essential footplate areas, reversing lever, gauge glasses, pressure gauges, even above the injector overflow. Continuing on towards Bracknell, we now passed over the un-romantically named, Whitmoor Bog crossing, where a small sewage works was located. The name was in no way a reflection of the works, but it never ceased to amuse me as a young man. Three further small level crossings came after Bracknell before joining the old original South Eastern Railway at Wokingham, in order these were Amen, then Waterloo, named I understand after a nearby Lodge, and lastly Star Lane.

We had been running with the steam pressure around 230/240 lbs and it was now time to start preparing for our scheduled stop on Reading Spur. This required a further reduction in boiler pressure, thus ensuring a quiet stand when we arrived. Turning the top of the incline at Earley, we drifted down the bank and on to the spur line. As we came to a stand, the WR conductor, Driver P. Talbot joined the footplate. Further back another WR man, this time a WR Guard, H. F. Simmons similarly climbed aboard.

Bill Neal insisted that Alf continue driving. This was a sensible measure, for whilst WR men did occasionally work Southern locomotives, they did not regularly handle Pullman rolling stock, with their own

distinctive vacuum brake valve which required a degree of braking expertise. The former Southern Reading depot, (old 70E), away to our left had officially closed in April 1964, however a number of locomotives were still to be seen on shed.

Despite the final arrangements having been prepared in advance, on the actual day we were advised of a last minute change meaning we were now to pass through Oxford station at just 20 mph, this was so that all the bells being tolled in the city of spires might be heard by those travelling in the funeral train. This hitherto unknown request put into question the right time arrival at Handborough, clearly some time in hand was required, so as we accelerated away from Reading General, the locomotive responded to Alf's call for speed in true 'Battle of Britain' spirit. Oxford was passed with time to spare, we even heard the bells on the footplate such was the smooth running of the engine.

Approaching Handborough, special instructions were in force that permitted the train to run non-stop through a recently installed set of facing points on to the Up line and into the station. A special 'STOP' board had been erected between the tracks to determine the exact position that the train should stop. Alf duly responded by bringing the train to a stand with the precision demanded. Incredibly too, the little station had been

transformed by the clever use of linen drapes covering all of the old tired, worn paintwork that we had seen only days previous.

After arriving, when all the mourners had solemnly alighted and the cortege departed for the church of St Martin's in Bladon, we uncoupled. Then, after being shunt released, we ran tender first to Oxford depot, 81F. The initial concerns that we had had about water and the conservation action that was applied on the day had worked admirably, as there was still plenty to spare when we stopped in the depot yard.

By this time, the special disc boards had been returned to their closely guarded mahogany box and stored away. After refilling the tender with water and shovelling forward coal for the return journey, we turned the locomotive and in the fading light ran light engine back to Reading General.

Standing on the 'Up Fast' line in the station, the WR pilot driver departed. The Chief Inspector then handed control of the locomotive over to me to drive back to Nine Elms depot and did the firing himself. Alf was left to drink tea and look on. What an end to an incredibly eventful day, I was literally 'chuffed'.

Following the event, I received a copy of a piece of correspondence from the Duke of Norfolk and addressed to the General Manager. The letter closed by saying, '"….. please thank any of your people I may have missed out, as naturally, I have not met all those concerned in a memorable week". Well that certainly included me, but it's the thought that counts. Later I received a postal order for the princely sum of 15 shillings (75p) for a job well done, those were the days.

Opposite page - Between Putney and Barnes. The crowd of onlookers was typical of what we witnessed at many places en-route.

Above - Still on the Southern, the train is seen approaching Wokingham.

Bottom - Now on the Western Region seen approaching Oxford.

Crossing over the temporary facing points onto the up line at journeys end at Handborough

34051 stationary exactly placed against the special stop marker.

Left - *From an obvious newspaper cutting, Alf and myself in somewhat pensive mood as we pose for the camera. It was extremely unusual to have such a high degree of media attention in those days and as the week leading up to the funeral passed by it began to sink in just what we had to do on the day! In those times I wore my coveted 'Engineman S.R.' brass cap badge that I still have to this day. Alf has a 'British Railways' brass and green enamel badge that became the general issue on the Southern following nationalisation in 1948.*

Ready to set off back to Oxford and eventually the Southern Region. This is the engine with the special headcode having been removed and in its place a single tail lamp.

Chapter 9

NAMED TRAINS

Apart from boat train, the times of which could vary, 'one-off specials' and the occasional 'Royal', Nine Elms had three duties involving regular named trains. (The 'Devon Belle' had ceased to run prior to my time.)

The Bournemouth Belle

The first of these was the 'Bournemouth Belle', itself a successor to the pre-war 'Bournemouth Limited'. During the late 1950s and early 1960s, the 'Bournemouth Belle' was worked from Bournemouth depot on weekdays although it was always a Nine Elms duty at the weekends. The introduction of 'The Royal Wessex' service in 1951, in connection with the Festival of Britain, had seen the weekday 'Belle' work transferred to Bournemouth whilst Nine Elms crews worked the 'new' train in both directions. Nine Elms Top Link covered the 'Belle' on Saturdays with Number Two Link, or 'Pilot Gang' as it was generally called at the depot, taking it on Sundays. In terms of who actually worked the train, there was no question of any particular crew being selected, it was determined solely by roster rotation and when it was your turn, that was it.

I have a few memories of working the 'Belle', the first, perhaps, a rather an odd one. On this particular occasion and having relieved the Nine Elms preparation crew at the top of No 11 platform, we were issued with a special stop order by the guard to call at Beaulieu Road station, a small country station situated in the middle of the New Forest. Apparently, as it turned-out, this was to allow Lord Montagu to alight there as it was his local station. The order was quite explicit, in that the driver should ensure that the third coach from the front should be stopped so as to give access to what was a short platform. When you have had a railway running across your land since the 1850's it's interesting what preferential treatment you receive.

A further recollection is of the practice of giving both the driver and fireman of the train a bottle of light ale when the train was stopped at Southampton Central. One of the Pullman stewards would come walking down the platform holding a tray with the two bottled drinks. We would consume them with relish. "God Bless George Mortimer Pullman". Of course, by today's standards, this would never be allowed, but the railway was very different then.

Another memory of the train is quite an interesting one. I had worked the service on a number of occasions and most of these were routine trips. However, my driver, Bill Turner and I were faced with a bit of a problem when in charge of the Up train on Sunday 17th March 1963. In the morning, we had worked the 11.30 am from Waterloo to Bournemouth West, stopping at Basingstoke, Winchester, and then numerous other stations on the way down. We arrived at Bournemouth West at 2.20 pm, then after being shunt released, ran light engine to Bournemouth Central. Here we left our engine, 'Standard 5' 73081, 'Excalibur', on the depot pit for servicing. I recorded that on the down journey, the engine was not steaming freely, possibly due to the poor quality coal.

After a meal break, we took charge of 'MN' 35030 'Elder Dempster Lines', a Nine Elms engine that I had worked on a number of times and knew well. Equally I had found it to be a good locomotive. We left the depot at 3.55 pm and ran tender first, to Bournemouth West ready to work the Up 'Belle' due away at 4.30 pm.

The first part of our journey was uneventful. After stopping and taking water at Southampton Central we continued the second leg of the trip making good time climbing the bank and passing Basingstoke with time to spare.

In those days the first piece of conductor rail encountered was on the Up local, where the line from Ascot was linked into the main line at Sturt Lane Junction, having coming off the Ash Vale line at Frimley Junction. A few miles further, at Pirbright Junction., saw the line from Alton similarly join the Up local. As you passed through Brookwood , there was a crossover from the electrified 'Up local' line onto the 'Up through' line, thus from that point onwards, there was a continuous conductor rail on both running lines leading all the way into Waterloo.

Incidentally, locomotives generally rode somewhat rougher over electrified lines, due, it was said, to the affect that electric units had on the permanent-way , this became quite noticeable once running over these lines. On this day however, as we passed through Brookwood and at quite a high speed I might add, there was a loud bang from underneath the engine. Bill looked at me with a puzzled expression on his face, and then, a little later, there was another similar bang.

I think we both realized at the same time what had happened, the ash pan hopper door, normally held in place by a locking catch, had somehow come open and was now coming into intermittent contact with the top of the conductor rail. The knock on effect was that as it short circuited the third rail, in was also blowing out the circuit breaker in the Electrical Control, thereby depriving both the section of line immediately ahead and behind of power. The control room operator at Woking would have been aware of the situation immediately and would have put the breaker back a couple of times in an attempt to restore the power, but he was not allowed to do this more than twice, not until someone made contact to explain the problem and the remedial action taken.

Even as we passed through Woking at 80 mph and with green signals ahead, we knew we would be stopped shortly. Sure enough, on approaching West Byfleet, the semaphore distant signal was 'on'. Up to now we had been running well and were in good time, but there was no way Electrical Control would allow us to continue while this was happening. West Byfleet's 'home' signal was expectedly at danger as we approached and we slowed right down, the signal cleared very slowly indicating that observation at the signal-box was required. Slowly we pulled forward, coming to a stand opposite the signal box where the signalman, now standing at the box window, could see what we were doing. We indicated to him that we understood the problem, so after checking the 'Up local' line was clear of trains, I climbed down onto the track. I had taken the 'rocker bar' with me and having inserted it into the hopper operating device, yanked the door closed and banged the catch in place behind it. The signalman

witnessed exactly what was happening and was already clearing his signals as I finished. Meanwhile on the footplate, Bill was observing both me and signals and had already set the train in motion as I climbed back onboard. Getting away from West Byfleet was not too difficult, the gradient slightly in our favour, even with a train of eleven Pullman cars. Bill then extended 35030, as he often had on other occasions to regain time, she responded well and we still managed to arrive at Waterloo right time.

The Atlantic Coast Express ('ACE')

In the early sixties Salisbury crews normally worked both the Up and Down 'ACE' trains. As the summer months progressed, in 1962, more and more holidaymakers made their way west from Waterloo to the scenic counties of Devon and Cornwall. This in turn, as indeed it had for many years before, required the Southern to provide extra trains in order to meet the demand, carrying both passengers and the essential buckets and spades. The 11.00 am 'ACE' departure alone was not sufficient to move the masses, so other departures were timetabled both before and after the traditional train's time of departure.

During this particular August period, Nine Elms crews took the 11.00 am 'ACE' and Salisbury men one of the supplementary services. This then was the situation that existed, I was twenty years of age at the time and my regular driver was Wally Finch in 3A, the 'Tavy Gang'. One day however I found booked along with Oswald George Coward, one of 70A's premier 1912 Top Link Drivers.

The thought of working the 'ACE' was not lost

Seen at the end of Salisbury's No 2 platform, 'V' No 30934 'St Lawrence' is hastily being prepared for the non-stop run with the up 'Atlantic Coast Express' in August 1962

John Bradbeer

on me, as I prepared the locomotive, 'MN' 35016 'Elders Fyffes' at Nine Elms. The normal time allowance was one hour for preparation and you certainly needed every minute. At this time of year, light engine movements between Nine Elms and Waterloo and return sometimes saw three, four or even more locomotives coupled together to reduce pathways. Equally on occasions there were but minutes to spare before departure, due to delays to these movements and the consequent uncoupling time standing outside Waterloo. Time just enough to back onto the train, couple up, receive details of the load and carry out the regulation brake test. Hectic did not describe the situation. Poor old Bill Cruse, the motive power foreman located at the top of No. 11 Platform, could be seen sometimes holding his head in his hands in sheer frustration.

On the day in question our start at 11.00 am went well. Despite the thirteen coach load, the engine responded immediately to my regular rounds of firing and with steam to spare we cleared the suburbs in good time. Woking then Basingstoke were soon in our wake as we continued on our way, 'Westward Ho!'. The locomotive was steaming freely and with the 'monitor' injector cut fine, I maintained the pressure at around 240/245lbs by use of the Ajax doors, leaving them half open but with coal filling the fire-hole after each round of firing to reduce cold air entering the fire-box. Suddenly I noticed something was amiss as we passed through Whitchurch North. The fire had started to burn ferociously and the safety valves lifted immediately. George Coward reacted at once, simultaneously shutting the regulator and opening the drain cocks.

He checked the water level in the boiler, that was clearly full, and then told me to blow the boiler down as we continued to run at high speed. My cut fine injector had in fact over-filled the boiler causing the engine to prime and we needed to reduce the boiler water level as quickly as possible. I set the blow-down in action whilst regularly checking the boiler water level using the test-cock on the water gauge. As soon as the water had dropped to an inch below the top nut of the gauge glass the blow-down valve was closed and with the injector working once again the boiler pressure was brought under control.

Observing the improved situation, George re-applied steam as we crossed the viaduct at Hurstbourne and started our climb on towards Enham and Andover Junction. Fortunately the engine did not appear to have suffered from this brief incident undoubtedly due to George's timely intervention. Another lesson learned as I remember, *keep checking the water even when things appear to be going well.*

The arrival of the 'ACE' at Salisbury was always quite a special moment. Time was of the essence once the train had stopped and whilst the tender was hurriedly filled with water, between five and six thousand gallons depending on the tender type, coal was being shovelled forward by the relieving Exmouth Junction fireman aided by some of the young Salisbury based firemen. The arriving fireman was always responsible for both the positioning and holding in place the huge water column pipe in the tender filler, no mean feat I might add, when hundreds of gallons of water was passing through it at considerable pressure. Some of the senior elderly Exmouth Junction men were never satisfied that the tender was full until water was streaming out of the filler point and flooding everywhere. As this was the normally expected event, I would to hang on to the column's swing-arm like a trapeze artist with my feet up when this was about to occur, in order to keep dry and not get washed off the back of the tender. Meanwhile whilst all this was going on, the incoming driver would be walking around the locomotive checking the valve gear for any sign of overheating and at the same time oiling the various parts of the loco in the short period available.

In next to no time whistles were blowing and flags waving, and our train from London was again on its way. Standing on the platform George checked his pocket watch with satisfaction as the 'ACE' now headed out of the station, climbing towards Wilton and the West Country that lay beyond. Undoubtedly it had been quite an eventful journey with the down 'ACE', but had turned out well in the circumstances with both a right time arrival and similar departure from Salisbury.

To my knowledge, early use of R E L Maunsell's incredible Class 'V' ('Schools') locomotives on the West of England route was extremely rare. As a 4-4-0 wheel-arrangement locomotive they were, from their concept, designed and built in the 1930s with other routes in mind. In fact during one particular period, none of the class were allocated to any of the depots on the South West Division of the Southern Region. Earlier years had seen them perform stunning work on both the Portsmouth direct and Bournemouth lines, that is until electrification of the former took place plus the requirement for larger locomotives on the latter, due here to increased train loadings. Once these changes took place, these fine locomotives were gradually transferred away and other than when required for special trains were rarely seen.

The year 1957 saw the beginning of a return to south-west metals of members of the class. Following 'modernisation' in terms of replacement rolling stock, namely the new DEMUs that were introduced on the Hastings service, previously services which had long been hauled by these remarkable locomotives. More then followed in the wake of the subsequent electrification on the South East division.

Rebuilt 'WC' No 34001 'Exeter' outside the shed at Nine Elms. The first of the 'Light Pacifics' it would remain in service until the very end of Southern Region steam.

Fortunately Nine Elms depot became a recipient of some of these early 'surplus' engines that were then soon utilised on diagrammed duties at the depot. One such diagram was 22 duty, that required one of these locomotives to work the 4.40 am stopping service from Waterloo down to Woking. Co-incidentally there were also twenty-two station stops between Waterloo and Salisbury on this duty. After a short recess at Woking, the train continued as the 6.36 am service down to Salisbury where we were relieved, it then continued on to Yeovil Junction where it terminated. The engine requirement facility at Yeovil Junction normally allowed the locomotive to be turned, oiled afresh and for fire and ash-pan cleaning. Equally coal also had to be brought forward for the return to London. This then is the background of events that occurred when in August 1962 the Up 'Atlantic Coast Express' failed at Yeovil Junction and the services of a 'Schools', 4-4-0, was then called upon to take the train

forward to Salisbury!

Meanwhile back at Salisbury on the day, the events at Yeovil Junction were unknown to us and with the Down 'ACE' well on its way we made our way to the end of Salisbury's Platform 2. There in the small Enginemen's cabin we had a welcome can of fresh tea and a quick sandwich before working back to Waterloo. During this period Nine Elms crews were also booked to work the Up 'ACE', so we had it all to do again and some food and drink were essential before the return trip. The 'ACE' was indeed the train of the day on the line and a great degree of effort was made by all involved to ensure its punctuality.

As the scheduled time neared for the up arrival, we were preparing ourselves for the crew change ritual when the telephone rang relaying the news. The Exmouth Junction 'Merchant Navy' had developed a hot bearing and could not continue. We were advised that a locomotive in Yeovil Junction yard was now bringing the train onward to Salisbury, although naturally with substantial delay. 'Control' also informed George Coward that a replacement locomotive was being prepared with all haste at Salisbury depot but it would still be some time before it would be available. Thirty to forty minutes later than scheduled the Up train arrived with 'V' 30934 'St Lawrence' at the head of the train. The footplate gauges revealed low water level and the boiler pressure of just 160lbs. The dejected Exmouth Junction crew stepped off the footplate, almost with an air of defeat, having done their best in the circumstances and no doubt believing that the locomotive would be changed on arrival.

A small degree of confusion arose as to who was actually going to uncouple and take the locomotive light to the depot, when suddenly out of the blue, George Coward asked me if had worked on the locomotive recently. I indicated that I had and that I considered it to be in good condition.

"Right" he said, "You get the fire, water and boiler pressure sorted out and we'll take the engine through to Waterloo". He then organised the support crew that were standing around to get shovelling coal forward and fill the tender with water. With the blower working overtime, pressure began to rise as I built up a rather depleted fire, whilst at the same time the injector raised the water level in the boiler. It was a hive of activity, although when we were ready to depart, we had coal stacked high, a boiler full of water and over 200lbs of steam. Needless to say thirteen coaches behind a 'Schools', even a good one, was going to be extremely demanding, but George Coward was a fine engineman with a wealth of experience. Slowly, we eased our way out of the station gradually picking up speed and once clear of the points at the east of station the regulator was soon in the second valve. Whether the fire had been cleaned at Yeovil Junction on the day I could not say, however I can record an extremely free steaming, 1935 built locomotive throughout the trip. No doubt the heavy working of the engine from the onset of the eighty miles plus journey up to London helped.

The real experience of George Coward only became evident to me after the event, for as we exited the tunnel he indicated to me that we would use the live steam injector 'cut fine' in preference to the exhaust steam injector. There was always a small amount of waste water before the latter would pick up, so bearing in mind the 'Schools' locomotives had only a 4000 gallon tender, albeit that we were running non-stop, the conservation of the water capacity was essential in the circumstances. Indeed a 'Light Pacific' with small 4500 gallon tender were sometimes near the limit when used on the Salisbury – Exeter route, so it was prudent to economise. Only occasionally would I briefly use the exhaust steam injector in order to wash down the

footplate and damp the tender coal.

Initially our progress was somewhat like a heavy freight train labouring on the 1 in 169 / 140 climb towards Porton. Our speed just a little over thirty five mph when passing through the station. As the gradient eased slightly so speed gradually increased, then having passed the old defunct Amesbury Junction, now renamed Allington, we finally turned the top of the bank just west of Grateley. Now with the gradient in our favour we raced down the bank towards Andover Junction with the regulator's position unchanged. Red Post Junction, dating back to the days of the old Midland & South West Junction's route to Cheltenham, was passed with clear signals ahead and as we dashed through Andover Junction the speedometer was registering over 80 mph! The bank ahead towards Enham intermediate signal did not pose the same problem as Porton had previously, such was the momentum of the train. Hurstbourne, Whitchurch North, Overton and Oakley were soon behind us and our concerns that we might get checked by signals approaching Worting Junction were unfounded as we passed without hindrance. On through Basingstoke at quite some speed, with a long lingering blast on the whistle, then onto the fast running ground beyond towards Farnborough. Even the outer colour light signal at St Johns was 'Green' and we again continued at speed unrestricted across the Guildford and Portsmouth trailing junction and on through Woking.

Our progress really was quite incredible, the locomotive, 'St Lawrence', like ourselves I felt, seemed to respond to the challenge, it truly was a most inspiring trip. George and I were both pretty mucky when we finally came to a stand, what with coal dust coming from the open back tender, the smoke and the sweat, whatever, nothing that a bucket full of hot water and soap wouldn't put right at the end of the day. Having arrived at Waterloo the portly figure of Stan Downes, the Motive Power Superintendent, was seen standing at the end of the platform by the buffers. Naturally he later had a few words with my Driver, a nod of appreciation for me was quite enough. Sadly for No. 30934, 'St Lawrence', that moment of glory was probably a swansong. For just four months later she was deemed surplus to requirements and withdrawn. Now reflecting upon that day, it was a privilege to be on the footplate and be a part in the final chapter of one of these magnificent class of locomotives, working alongside an equally special Nine Elms engineman.

The Royal Wessex

The 'Top Link' at Nine Elms was small in comparison to the 'Pilot Gang' but contained the best of the running work at the depot, which was a reflection of the principal of 'senior men senior work'! Equally the actual size of the link meant that the turns rotated with more regularity. Just looking back through my logs that I recorded those days and they reveal remarkable periods of continuous main line duties, day after day, on either the Bournemouth or Salisbury routes, the easier days being on stoppers down to Basingstoke.

As I indicated earlier we prepared our own engine for the down 4.35 pm 'Royal Wessex' that we worked to Bournemouth Central where we were relieved. The return working was the last Weymouth up to London. During the time I worked this particular train, we had on occasions a variety of motive power, including even LMR Black '5's, and even 'Caprotti' fitted 'Standard Class 5', most of them utilised from Branksome shed due to a shortage of locomotives. These engines arriving in the Bournemouth area either from Bath Green Park, over the Somerset & Dorset line, or from the Western Region. It certainly was interesting to have the chance of firing to something a little different.

Of these, the 'Caprotti' fitted locomotive was difficult at first, until we had her measure. Initially the engine seemed somewhat sluggish leaving Bournemouth Central and it wasn't long before we found out the problem once on the climb away from Christchurch up to Hinton Admiral. Whilst it initially sounded fine from the chimney, once the cut-off was reduced, the blast on the fire simply disappeared, although we were making moderate progress. We found the compromise was to work the locomotive no tighter than 40% cut-off in order to keep the fire lively. Thereafter she was fine coming up the bank to Basingstoke and onward to Waterloo. This was the only occasion that I worked on such an engine, what they were like in good condition I'll never know.

When working the 'Wessex' down one summer evening, we were making good time as we departed Southampton Central for our next booked stop at Brockenhurst. However, after passing Totton the semaphore distant for Ashurst crossing was 'on'. This was an extremely unusual event and was followed by Ashurst Crossing's 'Home' signal at danger.

Once we had stopped and I had damped the fire and reduced the boiler pressure, I made my way to the small crossing box. The signalman seemed surprised to see me when I knocked on the door, but told me that there was serious fire just the other side of Lyndhurst Road station and the Fire Brigade were on the line attempting to put it out. I informed him that I still needed to carry out Rule 55 and sign the train register, but at this he appeared to be slightly perturbed. Instead of being invited in, I was told to wait whilst he found an old newspaper and proceeded to spread pages of it over what was a highly polished linoleum floor all the way

'MN' No 35014 'Nederland Line' at the top of Waterloo's No 11 platform with the road set for 'Main Through', as we depart with 'The Royal Wessex' at 4.35pm. First stop Winchester, sometime in 1964.

from the door to his desk. I was amazed at the condition of the interior of the little crossing box, the brass block instruments were gleaming as was the wooden block shelf. He also insisted that I didn't spoil his neatly organised register, so first I had to wash my hands to placate his clear concern. He even came to check that I had not made a mess. His attitude changed immediately when he saw the entry, for I had written it all in my best Copperplate Script hand writing, he couldn't thank me enough. A little while later the telephone rang with a message that the line was about to re-opened, I made my way back to the locomotive and as we proceeded on our way we exchanged waves. That brief encounter probably made his day, it certainly made mine.

Above - *'WC' No 34025 'Whimple' awaiting departure from Waterloo at the head of the 4.22 pm FO extra Bournemouth service.*

Left - *'WC' No 34048 'Crediton' is prepared at Bournemouth Central shed alongside WR 'Hall' No 7914 'Lleweni Hall'.*

Chapter 10

THE DANGERS OF RAILWAY WORK

Throughout history the railway industry has claimed the lives of employees as well as passengers. Such was the nature work involving steam locomotives, that the law of averages would and did take the lives of a number of colleagues, even during my time on the steam. When I first read the classic book 'Red for Danger', by L T C Rolt, it became apparent that many of the accidents were caused by the simplest of mistakes, errors of judgement, duties badly carried out, whatever, but which then combined to escalate into something unimaginably catastrophic. But for every disaster , there was also a 'near-miss' factor, that might otherwise have ended differently had it not been for sheer good fortune.

I had several such 'close encounters' with fate. Other than the previously recounted fall off of the top of a 'Lord Nelson' boiler in 1958, the first really major incident that happened on the footplate was when working down to Salisbury one morning in 1962 on a stopping passenger service. After leaving Basingstoke our next stop was Oakley and where a number young ladies who worked mainly at the Overton paper mills would join the train. Up to this time, our engine, a Standard '5' had been working fine, giving no indication of what was about to occur. So after branching off the Southampton line at Worting Junction, we continued west towards Oakley with 'clear' signals. We approached Oakley perfectly normally with the regulator closed. At this stage the fire door was three quarters opened and the blower lightly applied, in order to reduce smoke as we ran in. The brake was also being applied as normal, when suddenly, just as we entered the short platform, a massive blowback took place. The ferocity of the flames were in fact comparable to that of the flame from huge blowlamp hitting the tender shovel plate with tremendous force. At the same time, the cab was instantly filled with both fumes and intense heat. Despite the immediate maximum use of the blower, the cab conditions could not be contained, it was only when we stopped did we get the dire situation under control on the footplate and I was then able to close the fire-hole door. Initially we both thought a tube had burst, but we soon found out the real reason; the smoke-box door was wide open. Under braking the heavy door had swung open and the air pressure entering the smoke-box then continued down through the tubes pressurising the firebox, the open fire-hole door had created a funnel for the volatile fire and air mixture. Clearly the smoke-box

door had not been secured correctly nor checked during preparation. The result of which could have been fatal in other circumstances. We were not responsible, as after signing on duty that day we were booked to relieve on an already prepared locomotive. In my particular case seconds before that I had been standing in front of the same fire-hole door before crossing the footplate to view the Oakley 'belles' waiting on the platform.

On a cold Boxing Day in 1962, I found myself booked along with Frank Morris. Whilst he was not one of my favourite drivers, we were to work a Boat Train down to Southampton Docks, later returning to Clapham Yard with the empty stock. Signing on at 4.30 pm it was understandably dark as we prepared the locomotive. The depot was also unusually quiet, with very few staff on duty as we moved out of the New Shed. It was clearly a case of 'help yourself' as we made our way towards the water column and coal hopper. With water taken we progressed to the small cabin normally occupied by the Pointsman, who also booked locomotives in and out of the depot, but at this festive moment was equally conspicuous by his absence. Snow and ice still lay on the ground as I climbed down from the locomotive to set the points in order to set back under the hopper for coal. The hand-operated points did not have that usual positive 'clunk' as they were pulled, so I stepped into the 'four-foot' to check that the point blades were correctly in place. A familiar 'creak' from the weight of a locomotive on the sleepers was the first indication of danger. I instinctively turned around to find the tender buffer beam bearing down upon me. I just had time to grab the coupling hook and raised my feet onto the brake rigging at the rear. Hanging on and shouting out, the locomotive eventually came to a stand. I made my way back onto the footplate and confronted the driver demanding to know why the he had allowed the engine movement back towards the hopper. 'I thought I heard you say alright', was his smug reply. Understandably I was extremely angry, not least because despite the fact that he had almost killed me, he failed to acknowledge or apologise for his deplorable actions. But that was the typical reaction of this arrogant man. Needless to say, that evening's work together was not at all conducive. I could say much more about this individual, but it is perhaps best it remains unsaid, for he is easily outnumbered by finer men well worthy of recollection.

Top left - *Jack Wicks and his Fireman, at that time D. D. Davis, on the footplate of 70A allocated Class '5' No. 73118.*

Centre - *An authority on all things associated with the original Bulleid locomotives was Engineman Alan Wilton. Founder member of the 'Blackmoor Vale' preservation society, he is seen here at Fareham in 1959 alongside Brighton crewed 'BB' No 34055 'Fighter Pilot' in 1959 .*

Bottom left - *Alf and myself on 'WC' No 34101 'Hartland, at Southampton Central in 1964.*

Bottom - *Exmouth Junction, '72A' man, Ted Crawforth: 'Smokey'.*

Chapter 11

PASSED FIREMAN

The rules, regulations and theory part of my driving test, took place just four weeks just after my twenty-third birthday in early October 1965. I was duly informed to present myself at Woking by 9.00 am, the actual classroom one of the temporary wartime control offices. Twenty years after their emergency here we were using the same wooden buildings to which staff had been evacuated in an attempt to afford a place of relative safety. Indeed they were to remain in situ many more years providing offices for various railway departments.

Inspector George Bolland was waiting for me. Always rather stern in nature, there was rarely a rare hint of humour with him, that could, on such an occasion, help put one at ease into the purpose of the day. Rules and Regulations in the morning, then after a mid-day break, the theory aspects of different classes of locomotive, brake systems, valve gears, boilers, defect identification, repair card, daily ticket returns and report writing.

It was normal practice for two senior firemen to attend the driving examination, a situation that would at least give one the opportunity to think about the subject being discussed whilst your colleague was going through the mill! But on this day I was alone and had to bear the brunt of continuous questions with little respite to regain a bit of steam, so to speak!

Even so, I thought the morning session went quite well, without too much pressure or difficulty over the many aspects of rules, regulations and signals. How many times I had read that rule book I couldn't say. Having said that, my mother could certainly match me, for she would regularly sit down in the evenings and take me through the various sections, detention at signals, protection rules, wrong line working, single line working over a double road, exceptions of passing signals at danger and many more. Unfortunately, any regular attendance at the extremely good 'Mutual Improvement Class' at Nine Elms, meant extra travel trying to accommodate it between shifts. Consequently in general I studied alone, but on occasions with the grateful aid of my driver as well as taking any opportunity to discuss aspects of the driving craft with other friends and colleagues.

The afternoon session came all too soon after lunch. Discussion on valve-gears and 'round the wheel' were always a protracted affairs, where is she taking steam, how to test for blows and knocks, how to isolate a broken valve spindle? It seemed endless at the time; whatever, we progressed and moved on to the other subjects to be covered. I became aware though that during my description of the functioning of the vacuum brake, the inspector appeared to be not really listening to what was a well rehearsed piece of mine. When I eventually stopped speaking there was a significant pause. Suddenly he responded by asking me to describe the workings of the small jet ejector, something I had in fact already done. Diplomatically I indicated that I had already dealt with the subject, but if he wanted me to go over it again I would. He curtly replied that it wouldn't be necessary. At the end of the day he checked his notes with some deliberation and finally indicated that I had passed this first part of the examination. Naturally I thanked him and as I walked out of the door I felt both relieved and extremely pleased.

Shortly afterwards, on 19th October, I presented myself at Waterloo to meet George Bolland, this time for the practical part of the driving examination. Making my way to platform nine I found 'WC' No 34018 '*Axminster*' at the head of the 9.30 am to Bournemouth with a load of 10 coaches equal to 335 tons. The booked footplate crew on the train were from Eastleigh depot. The driver was Des Holley, who, after I assured him that I was conversant with the route, retired to travel in the train. His fireman at that time was Ben Cartwright, with four years experience, quite a young man in those days. Whilst at the time of writing Ben is still working for South West Trains he is also a driver on the Mid-Hants Railway these days and continues his interest in steam locomotives along with many other retired loco-men from the past.

The start with 34018 from Waterloo was quite straight-forward, the first stop being at Woking. The engine was running nicely, in good mechanical condition with plenty of steam and made light work on the of the 10 coach train.

Just after milepost 31, near Deepcut, there was a Temporary Speed Restriction of 20 mph that I had noted and marked in my speed notices, this was duly observed as we proceeded down to Basingstoke. As such I was quite taken aback when a somewhat perturbed George Bolland tapped me on the shoulder and asked me where we had lost time whilst also checking his watch. I reminded him that we had passed over a lengthy speed restriction where we would normally have been running at 65 mph. He instantly

Engineman Ernie Harvey is seen here at Bournemouth West with 'WC' No 34026 'Yes Tor', I recall he kindly let me have the regulator on the return working that day.

relaxed, relieved we hadn't actually lost any time at all. At Eastleigh we handed the train over to the relieving crew and made our way over to the Up platform to work back to London.

We waited a short time before the arrival of the up service, this time worked by a Nine Elms crew. The driver, Fred Domm, was duly informed that I undergoing my practical driving examination and without any prompting was smartly back in the train with his Daily Mirror in his pocket. Fred's regular mate at the time was Mark Thom and we exchanged a brief hello before starting away. After Eastleigh, the next stop was at Winchester City, then Basingstoke, the subsequent climb up the bank to Litchfield was no problem at all with the engine working well. Leaving Basingstoke we had the gradient in our favour and the train speed easily increased. I made sure I drove the same as Alf throughout the whole examination. After stopping at Woking, George Bolland indicated that we would get off so I hurriedly went and found Fred, but before leaving I thanked both Fred and Mark for their assistance on the day.

I was somewhat surprised that we were not going to continue to Waterloo, however that was George's decision as the examining Inspector. Whilst standing on the platform he asked me what defects I had noticed on the locomotive which I would put on a 'Repair Card' when returning to the depot. I told him what I had observed and he seemed satisfied with my response. Again a dramatic pause, then, "Well I'm please to tell you that you have passed the examination and I shall inform the depot accordingly". Then he added a word of advice "Don't get too familiar with these fireman now that you are a driver"! Naturally I was extremely pleased with the day's work but his parting comment was difficult to accept, for as a fireman I had always had a good working relationship with my drivers and I was determined to continue in the same manner, whatever.

So approaching the end of 1965 I was almost at the end of my firing career. In next to no time I would be virtually back where I started as a young Passed Cleaner in 1958, albeit this time as a young Passed Fireman, preparing, disposing and ferrying locomotives to Waterloo for the ever diminishing steam-hauled main-line services. Despite the fact that I had signed for all the principal South Western Division routes, all so familiar to me, there was very little opportunity of ever driving on the mainline. At the end of 1965, just nineteen months of steam operation were left at and as each day passed, numerous locomotives were being withdrawn. Already locomotives were showing signs of deterioration and the high standards of maintenance were compromised by their impending fate. It was an extremely difficult time for the Region's dedicated enginemen and the fitting staff alike. I seriously considered it was perhaps all too much for me.

Despite becoming a Passed Fireman, I was asked if I would remain in the top link until the New Year of 1966. In the circumstances this was not at all unacceptable and enabled me to spend another three months with Alf who had become a special part of my life. Working together at all times of the day and night we had forged an unforgettable friendship and the opportunity to prolong the opportunity to put off the inevitable move onwards was fine by me. This extended time also enabled me to take stock of the situation and discuss the future with my good friend and mentor. The fact that Nine Elms was now officially destined to close, did not allow me to become an appointed driver at the depot as all footplate promotion had been frozen. This was intended to stop 'outsiders' using the depot's impending closure as a means of obtaining a coveted 'PTR' clause 14A 'redundancy' move, which in turn enabled such men the first choice of a move to other depots in front of men who had already registered a move many years earlier.

As such, I knew that once removed from the

top link I would on many occasions be back on the clinker shovel emptying fireboxes, whilst older in age, but junior in seniority appointed men, would be guaranteed driving turns. This was something that I was not prepared to accept, despite my great affection for steam and after discussing this in depth with Alf he reluctantly, but wisely, advised me to move on. The changes at the depot were there to be seen and there was no real future that would ever provide the same level of immense satisfaction that I had previously known.

The decision to move on was difficult, but entirely logical for my railway life was about to change forever whatever I finally decided. As such upon making enquiries at Arkwright Road, ASLE&F Headquarters, I found out that a driver's position would soon become available at Windsor & Eton Riverside EMU depot and I learned that I could take the position if I applied for the post.

I was thus appointed a Driver at the beginning of 1966 and sadly witnessed from a distance not only the final demise of steam, but also that of the Southern's long time freight operations, namely the closure of Nine Elms Goods, the marshalling yard at Feltham and numerous other yards including those in the Southampton area. The impending conclusion to the Bournemouth electrification scheme equally saw the introduction of colour-light signals replacing the long serving semaphore signals and the removal of virtually all the signal boxes along many routes. Even the Southern Region's identity and its associated green livery would disappear, as would the British Railway uniforms that we all took for granted. Whatever, I still count myself as having been both extremely fortunate and likewise privileged in observing and participating in almost the last decade of steam working.

But whilst one chapter closed so another opportunity would present itself. At the time I could

Arthur Camp and Colin Cottey are seen here alongside unidentified Merchant Navy at the top of Waterloo's number 11 platform in 1965.

Colin Cottey collection

never have envisaged where my career would eventually take me. The modernized railway certainly did not exactly fill me with enthusiasm. However the years between 1966 and 1990 were not so bad, and a 1970s move to Woking MT depot broadened the scope of work performed on Classes '33', '73' and '47'. Surprisingly the final fourteen years of my career saw a complete change, when I left driving behind and took a position with the new 'European Passenger Services' (EPS) based at Waterloo. I had always been fascinated by the

Maurice Boyce shares a joke with Alf Hurley whilst waiting for the 'Right Away' at Woking on 'West Country' No 34091 'Weymouth'.

concept of running through trains to the continent and seized the opportunity of fulfilling yet another long term railway interest. Within one week of joining 'EPS' I was in Paris meeting my SNCF counterparts and forging special friendships that last to this day. My arrival at Gare du Nord on that first day was somewhat akin to being back at Brooklands Road SW8 all those years ago in 1957. As I looked at the magnificent station I thought about my future and what might be ahead. Not steam locomotives this time but TGV trains, running on dedicated high speed lines, another dimension in rail travel. My initial mission was to identify all the driving tasks of a UK Driver to operate trains through the Channel Tunnel and continue on to Paris and Brussels, but that really is another story.

Top right - Inspector Tim Crowley, seen here on the footplate of 'MN' No 35008 'Orient Line,' at the end of the line in Weymouth depot, recorded during the last days of steam operation in 1967.

Bottom left - Two old friends Tim Crowley and Alf Hurley alongside a stranger to Nine Elms, 'Standard Class 5' No 73155. *P. Bassett*

Bottom right - Fred Prickett, an extremely knowledgeable Nine Elms Engineman, on the steps of now preserved 'MN' No 35028 'Clan Line'. *MNLPS*